Winning with
ETF Strategies

Winning with ETF Strategies

Top Asset Managers Share Their
Methods for Beating the Market

Max Isaacman

Vice President, Publisher: Tim Moore
Associate Publisher and Director of Marketing: Amy Neidlinger
Executive Editor: Jeanne Glasser
Editorial Assistant: Pamela Boland
Operations Specialist: Jodi Kemper
Senior Marketing Manager: Julie Phifer
Assistant Marketing Manager: Megan Graue
Cover Designer: Alan Clements
Managing Editor: Kristy Hart
Project Editor: Jovana San Nicolas-Shirley
Copy Editor: Deadline Driven Publishing
Proofreader: Seth Kerney
Senior Indexer: Cheryl Lenser
Senior Compositor: Gloria Schurick
Manufacturing Buyer: Dan Uhrig

© 2012 by Max Isaacman
Published by Pearson Education, Inc.
Publishing as FT Press
Upper Saddle River, New Jersey 07458

This book is sold with the understanding that neither the author nor the publisher is engaged in rendering legal, accounting, or other professional services or advice by publishing this book. Each individual situation is unique. Thus, if legal or financial advice or other expert assistance is required in a specific situation, the services of a competent professional should be sought to ensure that the situation has been evaluated carefully and appropriately. The author and the publisher disclaim any liability, loss, or risk resulting directly or indirectly, from the use or application of any of the contents of this book.

FT Press offers excellent discounts on this book when ordered in quantity for bulk purchases or special sales. For more information, please contact U.S. Corporate and Government Sales, 1-800-382-3419, corpsales@pearsontechgroup.com. For sales outside the U.S., please contact International Sales at international@pearson.com.

Company and product names mentioned herein are the trademarks or registered trademarks of their respective owners.

Printed in the United States of America
First Printing March 2012

ISBN-10: 0-13-284918-6
ISBN-13: 978-0-13-284918-0

Pearson Education LTD.
Pearson Education Australia PTY, Limited.
Pearson Education Singapore, Pte. Ltd.
Pearson Education Asia, Ltd.
Pearson Education Canada, Ltd.
Pearson Educatión de Mexico, S.A. de C.V.
Pearson Education—Japan
Pearson Education Malaysia, Pte. Ltd.

Library of Congress Cataloging-in-Publication Data

Isaacman, Max.

  Winning with ETF strategies : top asset managers share their methods for besting the market / Max Isaacman.

     p. cm.

  Includes indexes.

  ISBN-13: 978-0-13-284918-0 (hardback : alk. paper)

  ISBN-10: 0-13-284918-6

  1. Exchange traded funds. I. Title.

  HG6043.I833 2012

  332.63'27--dc23

                                 2011041196

Contents

Acknowledgments

Thanks to Research Affiliates (RA), BlackRock, Rydex, and the participating managers, for their guidance and help. Some of RA's research was covered in my book *Investing with Intelligent ETFs* (McGraw-Hill, 2008). Thanks to my friends and associates at East/West Securities and at White Pacific Securities: Echo Chien, Dr. Charles Chen, Benny Choi, Bob Angle, Monte Pare, Bin Yang, Diana Vuong, Aaron Small, Ming Hwang, Amy Guan, Zebo Huang, and Walton Lee. Also, I thank my editor, Jeanne Glasser; my agent, David Nelson; Dr. Abbot Bronstein; my wife, Dr. Joyce A. Glick; my children and their spouses, Jonathan Isaacman, Linda Burnett Isaacman, Carrie Isaacman, Roger Stude, and my step-daughter, Dr. Danielle Kaplan. A shout out to Nathan Stude and Harper Joanne Isaacman for arriving in the world and alerting us again to the fact that life is for both sprinters and long-distance runners.

Disclaimer: I own ETFs for myself and for my clients, and some of these ETFs might be written about in this book. There are always risks associated with investing in the stock and bond markets. This book does not guarantee you will make money in the stock and bond markets, and you could lose money. I am not making recommendations to any reader because an investor's ability to take risks must be taken into consideration before investments are made.

About the Author

Max Isaacman is a Registered Investment Advisor for individuals and institutions and is associated with East/West Securities in San Francisco. He was a Financial Consultant at Merrill Lynch, a Partner and Office Manager at SG Cowen, and a Vice-President at Lehman Brothers and worked in other positions in the investment community. Isaacman was a columnist for *The San Francisco Examiner* and wrote for many publications, including Delta Airlines' *SKY* magazine. He has spoken at CFA Institute events, CBS MarketWatch, Tech TV, the FTSE Global Index Conference in Geneva, Switzerland, and other places. *Winning with ETF Strategies* is his fourth book.

Introduction

The past ten years have been frustrating for stock market investors with the market moving mostly sideways, making it difficult to make money by buying and holding stocks. In a recent presentation, I told a crowd of individual investors that they can make money by buying Exchange Traded Funds (ETFs) and holding them for the longer term. They laughed, as if I was telling a joke. I wasn't surprised that people would be skeptical, but that's a good way to recognize the market bottom—when people laugh at the idea that the market will go up—and that is a good time to buy.

We know that markets fluctuate and always change, and often, markets do exactly what most people think they will not do. This sideways market could continue for a while, and in the mean time, investors and traders are making money or at least limiting losses in a variety of ways. Many use the new ETFs to go long or short, to trade currencies, to trade with a portion of their portfolio, to buy undervalued sectors or short overvalued sectors, and to use other strategies to trade and find ways to get varied asset-class exposure.

Market cycles have to be identified and considered. Before buying, you should know at what point in the cycle the market is at and where it might head. Markets move in cycles, and these cycles take years to complete. In this book, we show that according to research by Rydex/SGI Investments, in the past 113 years, there were 4 bull markets consisting of 42 years and 4 bear markets consisting of 71 years. Bull markets lasted an average of 10 years; bear markets lasted an average of 18 years. Even though there were fewer bull market years, the cumulative gains in the bull markets were substantial, and the cumulative losses or gains in the bear market years were slight. The bear years were more sideways markets than big down moves. Bear markets usually hang around, having periods of gloom interspersed with periods of hope. This is the market cycle we have been in for about ten years. Bull markets are usually vigorous and active, with big gains, sideways-to-down movements, and then more big gains.

Because there are more bear market years, you must get the best returns you can in those years, and you must try to cut down on losses. This can be attempted using a wide array of ETFs, such as sector ETFs, foreign country ETFs, non-stock market-correlated ETFs, and inverse ETFs, that enable you to short the market. History suggests that if you stay in bear markets, you will lose a little money, but bull markets return and are worth the wait. Unless the U.S. is in a long-term, irreversible decline—and there are those who think this is true, but I do not—history will repeat itself and there will be a bull market. The U.S. is a major player in the global economy and should continue to grow along with the international community.

Sections of this book explain how ETFs work, why they're the perfect securities for the current and future market, and which ones you should buy and why. To better understand ETFs, we examine where they come from and how they fit in this investment environment.

ETF strategies are varied and used in all sorts of imaginative ways. This book gives access to the strategies and methods of some of the most innovative money managers in the industry. The strategies and ideas of these selected managers can be useful, whether you are looking for someone to manage your assets or a portion of your portfolio or looking for fresh ideas from high-level professionals. These outstanding managers have been featured in top shows and publications such as CNBC, Bloomberg, Barron's, *The Wall Street Journal*, NBC, Larry Kudlow of CNBC's The Call, Erin Burnett of CNBC's Street Signs, Fox Business, TheStreet.com, Wall Street Transcript, and Research Magazine ETF Advisor Hall of Fame. Some people prefer managers with large sums under management and some prefer those with smaller amounts, so the managers are listed by amount of assets under management (AUM).

I've been a broker and advisor over the last 45 years and have seen many new types of securities offered. ETFs, in my opinion, are the most important securities released to investors, both individuals and professionals. I have written several books, and ETFs were always a major focus. I use and have used them for my own investing and for investing for my clients. I have spoken about ETFs to many groups over the years, including CFA Institute societies and The American Association of Independent Investors. I have spoken about ETFs on television and radio shows, including *Bloomberg* and *CBS Market-Watch*. I included ETFs when I wrote for the award-winning newspaper *The San Francisco Examiner* and when I wrote articles for many other publications.

1

The Evolution of ETFs

The Exchange Traded Funds (ETF) world has exploded since I wrote a book on ETFs about 12 years ago. Then there were only 32 ETFs, and the amount invested in them was about $65 billion. The original ETFs included the following:

- The Nasdaq-100 Index ETF (symbol QQQQ). This index is made up of the 100 largest domestic and international non-financial companies listed on the Nasdaq Stock Market, and the sizes are based on market capitalization. The portfolio is rebalanced quarterly and reconstituted annually. There are no portfolio managers deciding which stocks go into the index; instead, the stocks put into the index are automatic.

- The Dow Jones Industrial Average ETF (symbol DIA). The stocks put into DIA are chosen by a committee. The stocks are from companies that the committee deems the most important 30 companies in the U.S. economy. The average is the oldest market index at more than 100 years old. It is called an *average* because it originally was computed by adding up stock prices and dividing the total by the number of stocks.

- The S&P 500 Index ETF (symbol SPY). The SPY is comprised of the stocks of 500 companies that are chosen by Standard and Poor's portfolio managers. The S&P 500 Index is constructed to represent the U.S. economy, which is broken down into sectors. The portfolio managers decide which companies are the most important for each sector. Sector weighting is apportioned according to each sector's importance to the economy. For instance, if the managers conclude that the energy sector comprises about 30 percent of the U.S. economy, they will put about 30 percent of energy stocks into the index. The S&P portfolio managers don't attempt to put undervalued stocks into the index or find stocks that will go up; they just find stocks of companies that are important to the sector. Because the index is constructed to reflect general economic conditions, it is considered a passive index. This index is not made to be the most profitable for investors. Most of the other original ETFs were constructed along these lines. The S&P 500 Index is comprised of nine sectors. ETFs have been constructed for each of these sectors, such as the S&P Energy Sector SPDR (symbol XLE).

- The original ETFs included country ETFs, such as Japan (symbol EWJ) and Hong Kong (EWH). The indexes are constructed to basically reflect each country's economy and include stocks of the largest and most important companies in each country. Like the S&P 500 Index, the index is not constructed to outperform but to increase in value as the countries' economies grow.

- The original ETFs had an S&P small-cap ETF and an S&P mid-cap ETF. Like the other S&P ETFs, they are constructed of the stocks of the most important companies in each country. The stocks are chosen to reflect each country's economy, not to outperform a benchmark.

Objective of the Original ETFs

The original ETFs were not constructed to outperform any benchmarks, but were constructed to include companies that were the biggest and most important. As economies expanded, it was expected that the companies in the indexes would grow and the price of the stocks in the indexes would rise. It was accepted when economies slowed down that company revenues would also drop and stock prices would probably decline. The original ETFs were almost all cap-weighted or modified cap-weighted. Cap-weighted indexes have heavier weightings of bigger companies, and price moves of those companies have a big effect on the value of the index. Because of this structure, some index makers think that cap-weighting can have a built-in risk because bigger companies might have their greatest growth behind them. If a big-cap company's growth slows down (the bigger the company is, the harder it can be to keep growing), the company's stock price can be vulnerable. In market downturns, this type of company can be especially vulnerable and subject to declines such as the big-cap technology companies in the bear market years of 2000 to 2003. A cap-weighted index might overweight the companies that have grown and underweight smaller companies that have not grown as much. Some index makers think that indexes should have a mechanism that sells stocks when they get expensive and buy stocks when they get cheap. These index markers think that cap-weighted ETFs can perform the worst in good markets and decline the most in bad markets.

Cap-weighting indexes have performed throughout the years and have good points or they would not have been so successful. Cap-weighted indexes allow the bigger companies in their universe, which are usually the more important companies, to have a bigger weighting. This offers more exposure to more significant companies. Also, often the bigger companies in their cap-size have more financial muscle and might be better suited to weather economic storms. In the big-cap space, the bigger companies usually have more international sales, which is important in our global-trade world. The S&P 500 Index is essentially a big-cap growth index, and this asset class sometimes outperforms other indexes.

Development of New and Different ETFs

The market has grown dramatically, and there are now more than 650 ETFs with about $1 trillion invested. This growth should continue as ETF makers anticipate what investors need and create ETFs to fill that need. The need for new ETFs continues as markets change, and money flows into new ETFs when those ETFs perform. There are ETFs that offer investment exposure previously not available, such as currencies and gold. Before these new ETFs, there were few ways to invest in asset classes that were not correlated or had little correlation to the stock market. For instance, before the new ETFs and Exchange Traded Notes (ETNs), investors and traders could not buy currency, gold, or oil through tradable securities. Before the new ETFs, it was hard to invest in emerging markets. Investors and traders before could buy only cap-weighted ETFs and not fundamental, earnings-weighted, or other weighted ETFs.

Some of the new ETFs are constructed to outperform their benchmark indexes. These new ETFs are "intelligent" in that they are constructed to perform.

The launching of new ETFs is a major reason for the growth of the ETF market. Investors and traders want exposure to varied market segments, and this leads to the continual development of new ETFs. The market is limited only by the amount of foresight of the ETF makers and the demands from investors and traders.

New ETFs offer new exposure in other ways. One example is that before the new ETFs were launched, traders could not easily short the market and they could not buy the attempt to receive two or three times the daily performance of an index, either long or short. Of course, risk exposure is greater with enhanced ETFs.

The Launch of "Intelligent" ETFs

The new ETFs have opened the door to unique and profitable investment strategies that were once available only to the richest and most well-connected investors.

In June 2002, PowerShares Capital Management launched its Dynamic Market Portfolio ETF (symbol PWC). This was one of the first ETFs designed to outperform the S&P 500 Index. PWC has about the same sector exposure as the S&P 500 Index, but PWC has only about 100 stocks, unlike the 500 stocks in the S&P index. Instead of all big-cap stocks, which is what is held by the S&P 500 Index, stocks in PWC are small-, medium-, and large-cap stocks.

Instead of constructing an index that reflects the U.S. economy, which is what the S&P 500 Index does, PWC is constructed to outperform the S&P 500. In constructing PWC, PowerShares used its Intellidex method, which chooses stocks using many factors. One factor that Intellidex uses is to choose stocks that have a synergy when included in a portfolio together. For example, if Microsoft and Intel perform well when included in a portfolio, and Microsoft and IBM do not perform as well together, then Microsoft and Intel will be more heavily weighted in the index, and IBM will have a lighter weighting or may not even be included.

PWC outperformed the S&P 500 Index, and it took little time for investors and traders to recognize its good performance. They bought it and PWC grew. Other ETF makers saw the large amount of money pouring in, calculated the management fee that was being received, and prepared to launch their own ETFs.

Around the time PWC started trading, Rydex/SGI released its equal-weighted S&P 500 ETF (symbol RSP). RSP gives exposure to the S&P 500 Index without the big-cap stocks dominating the index because each name has the same weighting. The 500th company has the same weighting as the number one company, and the 499th company has the same weighting as the number two company, and so on, each company having a 0.02 percent weight. RSP outperformed partly because smaller companies often grow faster than larger companies, and the equal-weighted construction allowed more exposure to smaller companies. Investors and traders bought RSP, and the ETF grew rapidly.

RSP is a good buy for investors and traders who want a broad-based U.S. index, but do not want the dominance of big-cap growth companies possibly slowing its performance. An investor can buy RSP and hold it long term, and let the S&P portfolio managers figure out what replacements to make in the portfolio. There should be little, if any, yearly capital gains for holders of RSP, but there is a tax consequence when RSP is sold. If held over a year, the taxes are long term.

Significant money poured into these and other ETFs that performed. More ETF makers packaged and released new investment methods and asset class exposure through the unique ETF structure.

New ETFs Use Unique Strategies

Another provider of the new ETFs is WisdomTree, which is also an index developer. Some of its ETFs are dividend-weighted and some are earnings-weighted, which are different constructions from cap-weighted indices. WisdomTree studies show that dividend-paying stocks sometimes give support in down markets and can perform better in up markets than low- or non-dividend-paying stocks. WisdomTree and some other analysts think dividends are a good way to measure a company's health in that a company can use questionable accounting methods to hide poor earnings, but dividends are cash payments, and therefore a company must really make earnings to continue paying dividends. Dividends are not fixed and increase or decrease according to a company's earnings. Foreign ETFs especially can experience wide dividend changes year to year.

There are WisdomTree ETFs that give exposure to faster-growing foreign ETFs. Its Emerging Markets Small Cap Dividend

ETF (symbol DGS) has 50 percent of its portfolio in companies in Taiwan, South Africa, Thailand, and Korea. The dividend rate is high, at about 5.5 percent. The price/earnings multiple is 11 times, which is rather low. DGS is comprised of 23 percent mid-cap companies and 76 percent small-cap companies.

The WisdomTree Emerging Equity Income ETF (symbol DEM) has a high dividend rate of about 6.30 percent, and is comprised of companies in countries that have growing economies. Companies in Brazil and Taiwan comprise about 35 percent of DEM. The price/ earnings multiple is low at about 11 times. The companies in DEM have the following cap size: 46 percent large-cap, 37 percent mid-cap, and 15 percent small-cap. Another attractive ETF is the WisdomTree DEFA Equity Income Fund (symbol DTH). Companies in France, the U.K., and Australia make up about 55 percent of DTH. The dividend rate is at about 5.97 percent, and the price/earnings multiple is 11 times, which is low.

The investment management firm Research Affiliates (RA) also thinks that there are better ways to weight than cap-weighted, and provides ETFs that use its fundamentally-weighted strategy. The FTSE RAFI US 1000 Portfolio ETF (symbol PRF) holds about 1,000 U.S. stocks, mostly large-cap. It has a low price/book ratio of 1.5 and a modest 13 times price/earnings multiple. RA also uses this strategy in its FTSE RAFI US 1500 Small-Mid Portfolio ETF (PRFZ). The ETF is made up of small- and mid-cap stocks, has a reasonable price/ earnings ratio of 15.20, and has a low price/book ratio of 1.29. As far as foreign exposure, the FTSE RAFI Emerging Markets Portfolio (symbol PXH) has more than half of its portfolio in the fast-growing countries of China, Brazil, and Taiwan. PXH sells at a low multiple at just 11 times earnings.

The new ETFs have given options for investing in the S&P 500 Index, and at certain times, these other classes outperform the S&P 500. For example, in the 3-year period ending December 31, 2010, the S&P 500 Index returned a negative 2.9 percent. In this same period, the RAFI U.S. Small-Mid Cap ETF (symbol PRFZ) returned 7.5 percent, the Wisdom Tree Emerging Markets Equity Income ETF (symbol DEM) returned 8.9 percent, and the Wisdom Tree Small-Cap Dividend ETF (symbol DGS) returned 3.7 percent.

Other makers offer ETFs that give exposure to foreign markets, including emerging countries, Brazil, Russia, India, China (BRIC) countries, oil-rich countries in the Middle East, frontier countries, and other fast-growing countries. Other investment firms create ETFs that are not correlated to the stock market or bond market and are asset classes that were difficult to invest in before ETFs were created. Among these are ETFs offering exposure to gold, silver, real estate, and currencies.

A number of ETNs have also been brought to market. ETNs are not ETFs, and because of differences in their structures, there is usually a credit risk with ETNs. The new ETNs offer exposure to asset classes such as natural gas, oil, commodities, natural resources, and precious metals. ETF makers have brought out enhanced ETFs, which attempt to double and triple the daily return from chosen indexes. Of course, the potential risk is also doubled and tripled. Inverse ETFs have been launched, which offer the possibility of profiting from down markets, both on a regular daily return or on an enhanced daily return, with the risks being either regular or enhanced.

The ETF market keeps growing as new ETFs are released. Those that do not attract enough money fold, and new ones keep coming out. Different ways to use ETFs, according to the needs of investors and traders, keep increasing.

Investment Opportunity with the New ETFs

How can you make money in the market when so many choices increase your exposure choices to the point where you can't decide which ETFs to trade? For instance, you have to decide between buying a big-cap weighted ETF versus buying a small- or medium-weighted

ETF. Should you buy an equal-weighted ETF? Should you buy gold, short gold, or a short precious metals ETF?

This book clarifies what your choices are and helps you choose your best mix. You also read about what some of the brightest managers on the street are doing and their thought processes while making their decisions. ETFs are not just bought in a vacuum, but in relation to where the markets are and where they might go.

2

How Markets Move

Is this a good time to buy stocks, and where in the market cycle are we? Figure 2-1 shows that markets move in cycles. These cycles usually take several years to complete.

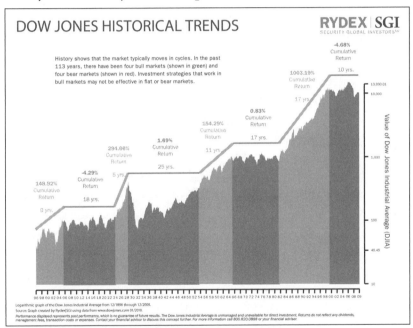

Figure 2-1 The market moves in cycles. (Source: Rydex/SGI Investment Management)

Figure 2-1 shows that starting in 1896, the market climbed for 9 years and had a cumulative return of about 149 percent, a good return. Then the market went sideways for 18 years. Money invested during these 18 years was dead money. Although the cumulative loss for those 18 years was only about 4 percent, the opportunity loss could have been substantial. If a person needed cash during this long period, he might have sold stocks out of necessity in one of the down legs and not had a chance to get back to even.

Opportunities to Trade Market Moves in Bear and Bull Markets

Markets make wide swings, which can be opportunities, especially since the new ETFs offer exposure in many ways.

In the years 1929–1954, the market moved sideways. It is no comfort to know that from 1926 through March 2007, the S&P 500 Index has had a compounded average return of 10.46 percent a year, including reinvested dividends, not counting taxes or expenses (Source: Standard and Poor's). That return is for more than 80 years. There are few investors who want to hold stocks for 25 years without getting some sort of return.

In 1982, the market started a 17-year bull run and made about a 1,000 percent gain. This was followed by a stock market decline, an implosion in housing prices, and a worldwide drop in the asset class values. Worldwide monetary liquidity had been created by extreme leveraging and the marketing of flawed assets, necessitating a period of deleveraging and concomitant market declines that continue to this day.

Figure 2-1 shows that there are steep drops and robust advances in secular bear and bull markets, often 10 to 20 percent moves. Market timing to take advantage of these moves, even with a small part of your portfolio, can improve performance. You can trade about 20 percent of your portfolio, you can trade stocks, and you can short those sectors you think are too high or buy those sectors you think are cheap. Holding a portfolio of indexes pays off if history repeats itself.

Some of the new ETFs are made for short-term trading, such as enhanced and inverse ETFs. Of course, there are greater risks using enhanced securities. Inverse ETFs attempt to return the inverse daily performance of an index. For example, an inverse S&P 500 Index attempts to go up about 1 percent on the day that the S&P 500 Index goes down about 1 percent.

With the new ETFs, you don't have to be in stocks when the stock market is going sideways or declining. Investors and traders can buy into asset classes that are low-correlated or not correlated to the stock market. You also don't have to buy and hold because you can trade easily using ETFs. In the sideways market we have been in since 2000, buying and holding broad market indexes hasn't worked well, although buying and holding certain asset classes, such as small- and mid-cap indexes, would have worked out better. In bull markets, such as the one that started in 1982, buying and holding almost any broad market index worked out. In 1982, you could have bought several broad market ETFs and held them for 17 years and received a good return, because that bull market went up about ten times. Investing and trading must be adjusted to the type of market you are in. For a buy-and-hold market, ETFs are often a better way than picking stocks.

Using ETFs to Maximize Returns in Sideways-to-Down Markets

Figure 2-2 shows 4 bull markets consisting of 42 years and 4 bear markets consisting of 71 years. The bull markets lasted an average of 10 years, and the bear markets lasted an average of 18 years. Even though there were fewer bull market years, the cumulative gains in the bull markets were substantially more than the cumulative losses or slight gains in the bear market years. The bear years were more sideways markets than big down moves. A factor in bear years is opportunity cost, because there are probably better places to put money than in the stock market. Bull markets are vigorous and active, whereas bear markets just sort of hang around with periods of gloom interspersed with periods of hope. This is the sort of market cycle we have been in for more than 10 years.

A secular bull market, or upward-trending market, occurs when each successive high point is higher than the previous one.

Start	End	Months	Years	Annualized Return	Cumulative Return	Annualized Std. Dev.
12/1896	1/1906	110	9	10.56%	148.92%	20.45%
7/1924	8/1929	63	5	30.44%	294.66%	17.30%
12/1954	1/1966	135	11	8.72%	154.29%	11.68%
11/1982	1/2000	206	17	15.09%	1003.19%	15.12%

A secular bear market, or downward-trending market, occurs when a trend does not rise above the previous high.

Start	End	Months	Years	Annualized Return	Cumulative Return	Annualized Std. Dev.
2/1906	6/1924	218	18	-0.24%	-4.29%	18.71%
9/1929	11/1954	304	25	0.07%	1.69%	24.96%
2/1966	10/1982	202	17	0.05%	0.83%	15.25%
2/2000	12/2009	120	10	-0.48%	-4.68%	15.61%

Figure 2-2 Four bull markets and four bear markets. (Source: Rydex/SGI Investment Management)

Because there are more bear market years, it is important to get the best return you can in those years. If you buy broad market ETFs that are weighted in a way that produces a good return, or good-performing sector ETFs, or ETFs in countries that have robust growth, or non-stock market-correlated ETFs that perform, you can make money in a bear market. Figure 2-2 shows that long-term return market bias has been on the upside, so it is worth staying in the market for the long term.

The Importance of Picking the Right Sectors

In good markets and in bad markets, the performance of different sectors varies widely. Often, there is a 40 percent yearly difference between the top-performing sector and the bottom-performing sector. Take a look at Figure 2-3.

Figure 2-3 The top and bottom sector performances. (Source: Standard and Poor's)

You can see in Figure 2-3 that there are big differences between the top and bottom sector performances every year. The difference was about 70 percent in 2000, for instance, and about 56 percent in 2009. The average difference between the top sector and the bottom sector for the years 2009 through 2010 is about 40 percent. An investor or trader, instead of picking which stock moves no matter what sector the stock is in, can concentrate on finding which sector moves the most and buy an ETF in that sector.

There are many ways to use ETFs to profit from the difference in sector performances. You can buy regular or enhanced inverse ETFs to short the sectors you think will decline and regular or enhanced ETFs to buy those sectors you think will go up. You can adjust your exposure in broad indexes by using sector ETFs. For example, if you are long SPY and are bullish on the energy sector, you can overweight it by buying an energy sector ETF, either regular or enhanced. Or, if you are long SPY and are bearish on the energy sector, you can underweight it by buying an inverse energy sector ETF, either regular or enhanced. Enhanced ETFs have enhanced risk. Because they attempt to return two, three, or more times the daily return of an index, their risk is also increased in the enhanced amount. If held for more than one day, enhanced ETFs run into compounding factors, which affect their longer-term performances.

One sector that can be bought as a hedge against inflation is the energy sector. The Energy Select Sector SPDR (symbol XLE), which uses the same stocks as the S&P 500 Index energy sector, is one of the ETFs that offers energy sector exposure. XLE's P/E ratio is about 14 times, which is reasonable, and as the demand for energy increases, the price of oil can increase and there can be a multiple expansion.

The drug and pharmaceutical sectors have good prospects and can be overweighted. Around the world populations are growing older, and this creates the need for more and better medications. The substantial research going into finding new ways to treat diseases and ailments creates new opportunities for pharmaceutical and biotech companies. Two good buys for this sector exposure are PowerShares Dynamic Pharmaceuticals Portfolio (symbol PJP) and PowerShares Dynamic Biotech & Genome Portfolio (symbol PBE). PJP is comprised of 30 U.S. pharmaceutical companies that are engaged in developing and distributing drugs of all types, and at 12 times earnings, is reasonably priced. PJP employs the PowerShares Intellidex system to select companies, which uses a variety of criteria, including fundamental growth and risk factors. PBE is comprised of 30 U.S. biotechnology and genome companies that are engaged in research, development, and distribution of biotechnology products, and sells at a 17 price/earnings ratio, which is reasonable for this sector. PBE also uses the Intellidex system to select companies.

Two other buys for health care exposure are Pharmaeutical HOLDRs (symbol PPH) and iShares Global S&P Healthcare Sector Index Fund (IXJ). PPH has a decent yield at about 3.25 percent and sells at a low price/earnings multiple of 11 times. The ETF is highly concentrated, with only 10 U.S. companies making up 94 percent of its assets. More diversified is IXJ, which includes companies in the U.S., Switzerland, Japan, and other countries. IXJ covers the health-care sector—including companies engaged in pharmaceuticals, health-care equipment, and services—and sells at a reasonable 14.47 times earnings multiple.

Risk Cycles and Market Returns

Is this a good time to buy stocks, and where in the cycle are we? Figure 2-4 offers some perspective.

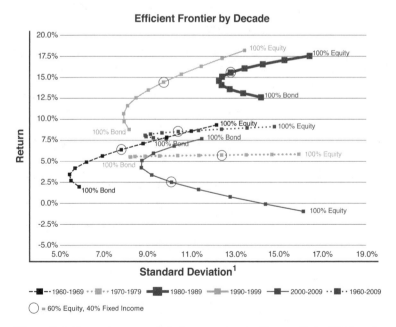

Figure 2-4 The performance of stocks versus bonds. (Source: Rydex/SGI Investment Management)

Stocks are riskier than bonds, so stock buyers expect more reward for taking more risk. Stocks usually outperform bonds, especially over long time periods. Figure 2-4 shows how stocks performed compared to bonds over several 10-year periods. The figure shows six "fishhook" performance diagrams of a portfolio of stocks and bonds. There are boxes on each diagram, each box showing the difference of a 10 percent mix of stocks and bonds in the diagrams. The circle in each fishhook represents a mix of 60 percent stocks and 40 percent bonds.

There are no guarantees in the stock and bond markets, but bonds are relatively safer than stocks. With stocks, there is no price guarantee, and they sell at the price of whatever people will pay for them. Bonds are different in that if bonds are held to maturity and the company has the resources, the bonds will be paid off.

Stocks outperformed bonds in all the 10-year periods shown in the fishhook graphics until the 2000–2009 period. In that decade, the performance is inverted and bonds outperformed stocks. A stock investor would have about broken even, and a bond investor would have made about 7.5 percent on average per year. In the past 100 years, there have been short periods when bonds outperformed stocks, but over longer periods, stocks have outperformed bonds. In the 1960–2009 period, which is shown in Figure 2-5, stock investors were rewarded for taking more risk as stocks outperformed bonds.

Almost every investment beat stocks over the last 10 years. Treasury bonds, silver, gold, platinum, oil, junk bonds, the 10-year Treasury bill—all of these had a better return than the stock market. Investments have cycles, and outperforming asset classes do not outperform indefinitely. Usually when people have given up on an asset class, the assets are selling the cheapest. History suggests it's time for the stock market to outperform again.

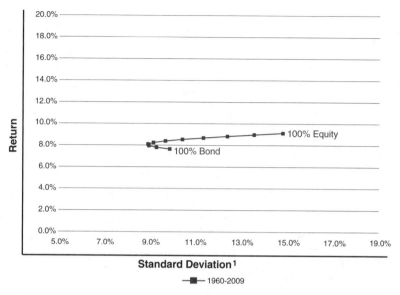

Figure 2-5 Stocks outperform bonds. (Source: Rydex/SGI Investment Management)

3

Long-Term and Short-Term Market Timing and Investing

The market that we've been in for the last 12 years or so has made traders of us all—we simply can not just buy and hold without making periodic portfolio adjustments. There are short-term and long-term considerations, and many investors have started using market timing for their buys and sells. Many others use portfolio adjustment rules as a way to enhance returns and lower risk. Different strategies are explored in this chapter.

The Risk and Reward of Market Timing

Many investors and traders use market timing to take advantage of market volatility, and Figure 3-1 shows why. Figure 3-1 shows the results of investing $1.00 in the S&P 500 Index in 1966, and Figure 3-2 shows the return over a 44-year period with three different scenarios:

- If you had been out of the market on the best five days each year
- If you had been out of the market on the worst five days each year
- If you had simply held the index through the good and bad days of each year

The Good, the Bad, and the Beautiful

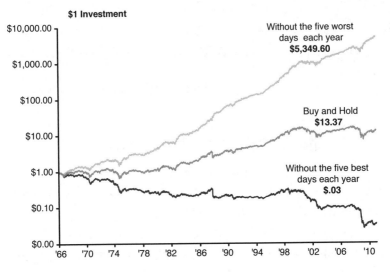

Figure 3-1 Under three different scenarios, a dollar invested in the S&P in February 1966 would have produced very different sums by the end of 2010. (Source: Birinyi Associates, Inc.)

Year	Annual Performance	Without Five Best Days	Without Five Worst Days	Year	Annual Performance	Without Five Best Days	Without Five Worst Days
1966	-12.86%	-21.34%	-3.27%	1989	27.25%	14.79%	46.49%
1967	20.09	11.66	28.67	1990	-6.56	-17.82	7.42
1968	7.66	-1.16	15.59	1991	26.31	10.05	41.93
1969	-11.36	-18.43	-4.08	1992	4.46	-2.95	12.60
1970	0.10	-13.65	13.89	1993	7.06	-0.90	16.03
1971	10.79	-0.06	19.40	1994	-1.54	-9.16	7.64
1972	15.63	9.31	22.49	1995	34.11	25.14	42.90
1973	-17.37	-27.23	-5.97	1996	20.26	10.17	34.99
1974	-29.72	-42.28	-18.06	1997	31.01	11.46	55.21
1975	31.55	18.56	45.97	1998	26.67	4.52	55.96
1976	19.15	9.83	28.70	1999	19.53	3.98	35.31
1977	-11.50	-17.30	-4.72	2000	-10.14	-25.28	8.64
1978	1.06	-12.63	12.88	2001	-13.04	-28.53	5.11
1979	12.31	2.17	24.07	2002	-23.37	-39.30	-7.84
1980	25.77	11.05	43.64	2003	26.38	8.79	45.38
1981	-9.73	-17.24	0.99	2004	8.99	0.70	17.81
1982	14.76	-5.29	30.80	2005	3.00	-5.02	11.02
1983	17.27	5.12	28.89	2006	13.62	3.38	23.47
1984	1.40	-10.64	8.26	2007	3.53	-9.43	20.16
1985	26.33	15.17	34.64	2008	-38.49	-58.89	-5.54
1986	14.62	3.41	34.30	2009	23.45	-4.04	57.37
1987	2.03	-20.09	60.18	2010	12.78	-4.31	33.79
1988	12.40	-2.70	35.11				

*Through May 21

Birinyi Associates Inc.

Figure 3-2 The annual changes in the benchmark average under the three scenarios for every year since 1966. (Source: Birinyi Associates, Inc.)

The buy-and-hold strategy would have returned $13.37, which is a decent return. If you had missed the five best days each year, you would have had a very poor return, with only $.03 left on the invested dollar. But if you had missed the worst 5 days each year, you would have had a great performance with the $1.00 being worth $5,349.60.

Why is it so bad to be in the market on down days? Down days are often sharply down. Up days give investors a sense of well being, investors relax, the world is okay, one grows richer, and one gets a sense of contentment, even euphoria. Up markets drift higher. Down markets, on the other hand, are sharp and scary. Fear tops greed as a motivating factor and people throw in the towel and sell as fast as they can, their hands shaking.

There are big differences in performances of each year in Figure 3-1. For instance, 1987 was essentially a flat year. But if you had missed the five best days you would have been down about 20 percent that year, and if you had missed the five worst days you would have been up about 60 percent. In 1975, the market was up more than 31 percent, and without the best five days an investor would be up only about 18 percent. An investor who was not in the market on the five worst days would be up almost 46 percent.

In bear and bull markets, there are sharp short-term moves, and market timing with a small part of your portfolio can increase performance. You can trade individual stocks or use ETFs to short those sectors you think are high or buy those sectors you think are cheap. Enhanced ETFs maximize exposure and can be used as regular or inverse. Inverse ETFs attempt to return the inverse daily performance of an index. For example, an inverse S&P 500 Index attempts to return one percent on the day that the S&P Index goes down one percent.

Using the new ETFs, you don't have to be in stocks when the stock market is going sideways or declining. Investors and traders can buy asset classes that are low-correlated or not correlated to the stock market. In the sideways market we have been in since 2000, the buy-and-hold strategy hasn't worked very well. In bull markets, such as the one that started in 1982, buy-and-hold worked. In 1982, you could have bought broad market indexes and received a good return for holding them for 17 years because that bull market went up about 10 times.

Long-Term Investing Using Indexes

There has been much discussion about buying and holding stocks. There is a question about whether that strategy has ever worked, even in good markets. We live in a continuously changing world, and what reality was yesterday quickly fades; the present is upon us. What does this have to do with investing and making money? Actually, plenty. We invest in companies and they constantly change, having to keep up with the demands of the marketplace. When they falter, they are quickly left behind.

I live in San Francisco, and hanging on the wall at my gym are photographs of downtown San Francisco in the early 1900s. The first photo, taken in about 1905, shows people walking on crowded sidewalks, passenger-filled cable cars rolling on tracks in the middle of the street, and horse-drawn buggies packing the streets. The next photo, taken several years later, shows the same downtown scene, the wagons with their bridled horses again filling the street, but also a few box-shaped automobiles, their tops down, looking strange. People probably looked at the autos as a novelty, as people walked on sidewalks, and rode in buggies, tugging on their horses' reins. The next photo showed buggies and many more cars on the street, the next photo showed a lot of cars and a few buggies, and the next picture showed a street filled with cars, and the horse-drawn buggies were gone.

The surprising thing was the length of time between the first photograph and the last. Was it 25 years or so? No, it was just about 15 years. It took about 15 years for our mode of transportation to completely change. Change is also true more recently. Only 20 years ago we barely used computers, and now we can't operate without them. Nobody used cell phones about 15 years ago. Remember looking for a public phone and putting in a quarter?

What does this have to do with investing and why it is better to buy indexes than individual stocks for long-term investments?

Well, if you had been investing back in 1900, you might have bought stocks in buggy whip companies, what with horse-drawn buggies being the primary mode of transportation, assuming that people would need transportation and more buggies would swamp the streets. You might not have seen that a buggy whip company investment would become worthless unless the company diversified and changed.

The idea that yesterday's modern investment might be tomorrow's dinosaur is discussed in an article by Jason Zweig (*The Wall Street Journal*, WSJ.com, February 14, 2009, "1930s Lessons: Brother Can You Spare a Stock?"), in which he cites a study that shows that after the stock market collapse in 1929, the only industry to have positive returns from 1930 to 1932 was logging. This was partly because logging companies made matches, which were important back then. As the years passed, matches became less important, and companies that made only matches became extinct, much like the disappearance of buggy whip companies.

When the stock market rebounded in 1933, companies that offered cheap vices made the best returns. These companies included tobacco products, sugar and confectionary products, and fats and oils. In those hard times, people bought things that made them feel better. Some of the industries that did well in the 1930s are extinct or barely exist today, such as leather tanning and finishing.

If you buy and hold stocks and don't pay attention to those stocks, you are at risk as times change. But if you hold indexes, the index portfolio managers make the changes that conditions warrant.

The Reason to Buy Indexes for Long-Term Investing

Instead of holding stocks for the long term, hold indexes in the form of ETFs, and the portfolio managers will make changes as economic conditions and industries change. For a broad-based, long-term investment, for instance, buy an S&P 500 Index ETF, such as SPY or IVV, or buy a fundamentally-weighted ETF, such as PRF or PRFZ. SPY or IVV offers industry diversification, because those ETFs are broken into nine sectors. The more important a sector is to the U.S. economy, the greater weight the sector will have in the index, and as its importance changes, weightings will be adjusted. PRF and PRFZ also offer industry diversification through their weighting formula.

You also get low-cost money management with these ETFs. The S&P 500 Index portfolio managers meet monthly to keep up with corporate events, and make changes in the index when necessary. The changes are frequent. Between 1964 and 2000, there were about 20 company changes a year in the index.

ETFs are tax efficient. Because of the creation and redemption process, there are usually few capital gains passed on to holders. Broader-based ETFs have had and are expected to have little, if any, capital gains. The difference between your cost price and your sell price is a taxable event. If you hold an ETF longer than a year, it is a long-term capital gain or loss.

4

Understanding Index-Weighting Choices

The S&P 500 Index was launched in 1957 and has grown to be the best known and most widely followed U.S. stock index in the world. Capitalization (cap) weighting is simple; it weights a company by the number of shares outstanding multiplied by the company's market price. The effect of cap weighting is that the larger the company, the more effect it has on the index. Because a market cap is partly created by the price of the stock, the market is essentially valuing a company, which affects an index because of the weighting a company is given.

The cap-weighted method is more than 50 years old, and through the years, there have been critics of this method. Criticism includes that the market cap is related to market price, and if a stock has a high price, it might be overvalued. The market-cap method then can over-weight the overvalued companies, because the higher the market price and number of shares out, the more weight a company has in the index. Conversely, the opposite can happen. The lower valued stocks can be too cheap, resulting in less of these cheap stocks going into the index. This can result in the index under-weighting the undervalued companies and over-weighting the overvalued companies.

If a stock is in favor, buyers might drive the stock up to double its starting price. The index, to keep its weighting method, has to increase its holding of that stock. This might not be the best time to buy more of this stock, because if you were trading the stock at some time, you would probably lighten up as the stock climbs. But this is how cap-weighted indexes are constructed. Cap-weighted indexes decree buying more stock as the stock increases in price.

Cap-weighting indexes have rebutted that unless one can say what the true fair market value of a stock is and unless it can be established which companies are overvalued and which are undervalued, the perceived shortcomings of cap-weighted inefficiencies are interesting and may have some validity, but are basically useless.

Is Cap Weighting the Best Way to Weight ETFs?

How indexes should be constructed is a disputed issue for institutional investors, individual investors, and traders. Cap-weighted ETFs might be the most widely held as far as assets under management. But cap-weighted ETFs have come under criticism because it is argued that the method might overvalue the biggest stocks and undervalue the smaller stocks that can lead to larger losses and smaller gains. According to John C. Bogle (founder of the Vanguard Group) and Burton G. Malkiel's (an economics professor and author of *A Random Walk Down Wall Street*) article "Turn on a Paradigm?" (*The Wall Street Journal,* June 27, 2006, Page A14), even though there are new ways to weight indexes, cap-weighting has stood the test of time and is still very valid.

Two economists, among others, think there are better ways to invest than just broad-based, cap-weighted indexes. Eugene Fama, Professor at the University of Chicago, and Kenneth French, Professor at Dartmouth College, suggest there could be higher returns in indexed portfolios of low price-to-book-value ratio stocks. The economists also favor small-cap stocks. Rob Arnott of Research Affiliates (RA) proposes that indexing by weighting stocks by fundamental factors such as sales, earnings, and book values is more effective than cap weighting. Dr. Jeremy Siegel of WisdomTree proposes that an effective way to weight indexes is according to the amount of dividends that companies pay. These index providers and professors propose that fundamentally weighted indexes are the best way to invest.

Mr. Bogle and Mr. Malkiel are of the opinion that cap-weighting indexes has worked well and will continue to be effective. They agree that fundamentally weighted indexes have outperformed cap-weighted indexes during certain years, but this does not mean that cap-weighted indexing is flawed. They point out that cap weighting has done well for its investors for the 30-plus years that they have been available. They have done so well that investors have poured more than $3 trillion into them. Cap-weighted indexes have gotten better returns than investors got before, when they could invest in only actively managed mutual funds.

Also, expenses for alternatively weighted ETFs can be higher than for broad-market, cap-weighted ETFs. Broad cap-weighted ETFs, such as those replicating the S&P 500 Index or the Dow-Jones U.S. Index Fund, usually have expenses of about 10 to 20 basis points. The expenses in fundamentally weighted ETFs are sometimes higher and can be 75 basis points or more.

Mr. Bogle and Mr. Malkiel also point out that fundamentally weighted indexes can incur higher and more frequent transaction costs. In a dividend-weighted index, for example, if one of the companies increases its dividend, then this company has to have a greater weight in the index. The manager has to buy more stock in the company and he has to sell stock in another company. Another occurrence is when a stock increases in price and its fundamentals, such as book value or cash flow per share, remain the same, so a fundamentally weighted index portfolio manager has to sell stock to reduce its weight in the index. This can occur often, causing the ETF to realize a profit.

Mr. Bogle and Mr. Malkiel point out that fundamentally built indexes tend to favor heavier inclusions of value stocks. Fundamental indexing weights according to factors such as high dividends or low book value, and companies have to improve these fundamental factors to have increased weighting in the index. Also, factors such as higher dividends or lower book value are value considerations, thus causing fundamental indexes to have more value stocks compared to cap-weighted indexes.

Cap-weighted proponents often conclude that fundamental portfolios will outperform when small-cap stocks and value stocks are in favor. Ibbotson Associates has compiled numbers that determine there have been long-term excess returns from dividend-paying, value, and small-cap stocks. But these returns can be over-stated because fees, taxes, and other expenses were not taken into account. There are times when value portfolios do well, and there are other times when growth portfolios outperform. Value portfolios generally performed better than growth portfolios from the late 1960s through 1977; however, there was little difference between the portfolios in 1977 through 2006.

There is no certainty that any one portfolio construction, be it cap-weighted, dividend-weighted, fundamentally weighted, buyback-and earnings-weighted, or another method, will work in any market, at any time. The index style has to be chosen in the context of the overall market atmosphere.

Are Markets Efficient?

The efficient market hypothesis tries to explain why markets perform the way they do and what markets will do in the future. The hypothesis claims that a stock price reflects all the available information for a company, and therefore, this price is correct and the markets are always correct. Markets are rational, the theory goes, information always changes, and the market price reflects the information as it is released and digested by market participants.

The efficient market model does not solve problems and it raises more questions. If a company, for instance, announces earnings that exceed estimates and its stock rises, should a trader or investor rush in and buy the stock? Or, should a trader short the stock, figuring that the news is out, and the stock's next move is down? Wherever the stock price goes, it is considered the correct price by those who believe in the efficient market theory. The market price is rational and reflects all information, both widely known and little known information.

If the efficient market hypothesis is correct, then cap weighting is the most efficient and logical way to weight indexes. Cap weighting implies that the markets are right and that stock prices reflect the rational state of a company's worth. If a stock is selling at 20 times earnings, it is justified, just as if a stock is selling at 50 times earnings. As a stock increases in price, its cap weighting grows, and more of the stock is added to the index.

Many analysts think that the stock market is not rational, and that there is much more that goes into a company's stock price than the information about that company. This would mean that cap weighting could be flawed, because as a company grows, it has a heavier weight in the index. As a company grows in market cap, because of its stock price, it may be overvalued and heavily weighted in a cap-weight portfolio at just the wrong time.

Maybe the efficient market theory came into existence because people cannot always beat the market, and this theory gives them an excuse if they lose money: Investors or traders can say that they did not know enough. You must know everything, and if anything is missing, you will be wrong.

Which Is Better: Cap Weighting or Alternatively Weighting?

This question is debatable. Some alternatively weighted ETFs have outperformed cap-weighted ETFs some of the time. Some say many alternatively weighted ETFs have been out for only about five years, and that is a short time to measure what will happen in the future and to conclude the superiority of one way to weight over the other.

Investors and traders still have to ask how much risk they want to assume, what size of capitalization exposure they want, in what sector they want exposure, in what region or country, and they also have to decide whether they want inverse exposure or enhanced exposure. They must determine what sort of market they are investing in plus other factors. When considerations like these are resolved, and the investor's risk and reward profile is clear, the investor can research the various ETFs to find those that fill their needs. How ETFs are weighted is one of the important factors in making investment and trading choices. An investor can clearly favor one way of weighting over another, or might use several index-weighting choices.

5

Fundamental Indexing

Rob Arnott of Research Affiliates (RA) does not believe that markets are wholly efficient or that markets are entirely rational, and he says that his conclusions are supported by strong empirical evidence and the growing body of work in behavioral finance.

He asks a question about the validity of cap-weighted methodology: "Cap-weighting claims that the market price is accurate, but if market price does not equal fair market value, how big is the difference?" Arnott says that analysts try to analyze the next quarter sales and earnings and are often off the mark. If they cannot accurately judge the next quarter's earnings, how can they judge what earnings will be two or three years out? The fair market value of a company should reflect its earnings potential decades into the future. If market participants agree that price differs from fair value, and cap-weighted indexes are based on market value, mathematically cap weighting structurally over-weights the overvalued and structurally under-weights the undervalued.

Arnott concludes that in a cap-weighted index, most of the money is in over-weighted companies because the index is over-weighting these companies, and this creates a built-in performance drag, or what RA terms "negative alpha." Arnott's research is dedicated to breaking the link between portfolio weight and stock price, which frees a portfolio from owning more of stocks when they are expensive and owning less when they are cheap.

RA says that freeing a portfolio from this potential performance drag by building a portfolio according to non-price weighted

measures—in RA's case, by the fundamental size of a company—
enhances performance significantly. RA created its "Fundamental
Index" (RAFI) in 2004. RA says the reason its alternative to cap-
weighting indexing has blossomed is the simplicity of its concept
and the success RAFI has had in its performance over cap-weighted
indexes.

For instance, RA has constructed indexes that are replicated
by mutual funds and ETFs, such as the PowerShares FTSE RAFI
US 1500 Small/Mid-cap ETF (symbol PRFZ) and the PowerShares
FTSE RAFI US 1000 ETF (symbol PRF). PRF tracks the performance of the 1,000 largest U.S. companies, based on four measures
of firm size: book value, cash flow, sales, and dividends. The key point
is that the RAFI strategy measures and weights the portfolio based
on the largest companies, not the largest stocks according to market
capitalization. The RAFI fundamentally weighted portfolio is rebalanced and reconstituted annually. PRFZ tracks the performance of
1,500 mid-cap and small-cap U.S. equities, based on the same four
measures of firm size.

According to *Morningstar*, during the five years ending in December 31, 2010, PRF, which was the first RAFI fundamental ETF offering, had an annual return of 4.3 percent. The companies in the index
are all large-cap companies, which is similar to the S&P 500 Index.
PRF performed about 2 percent better in this time frame than the
S&P 500 Index. The PowerShares FTSE RAFI Developed Markets
ex-US ETF (symbol PXF), which fits into the foreign large-cap value
category, for the three-year period ended December 30, 2010 and
returned a negative 5.8 percent. This was a better performance than
the MSCI EAFE index, which returned a negative 7.0 percent.

On a three-year basis, PRFZ also outperformed the S&P 500
Index. The more appropriate benchmark for PRFZ is Russell 2000,
which is a small-cap index. According to RA, PRFZ beat the Russell
2000 index since its September 2006 launch date.

Fundamental indexing and other alternative weighting methods do not guarantee profits or over-performance of cap-weighted indexes. There are times when the stock market is more of a momentum, growth-led market, and at that time, cap weighting might outpace other weighting. This is true in stock market bubbles. RA thinks this is because cap-weighted indexes keep riding the high-flying groups, such as the biotech stocks of the early 1990s or the dot-com Internet stocks of the late 1990s, to large portfolio weightings. Studying more than 200 years of market experience gives RA comfort that the next bubble ends the same way as the previous bubbles and the fundamental index investors benefit.

Comparing Equal-Weighted Indexes and Cap-Weighted Indexes

One of the first ETFs offered was the S&P 500 Equal Weight ETF, brought out by Rydex (symbol RSP). Each of the 500 names in RSP has a 0.2 weighting, and the selection committee rebalances the portfolio quarterly.

According to analysis by RA, in the years 2001–2005, the equal-weighted index was up 51 percent. The S&P 500 Index was up only 1 percent. It's worth looking at why there was such a big difference. In 2001, the S&P 500 was heavily weighted in companies that had the highest price/earnings multiple in history. In January 1995, the S&P 500 Index was invested in only about 11 percent technology. In March 2000, this sector weighting had grown to about 34 percent. Having that much in technology created built-in risk. But technology was on a roll, and many traders and investors kept piling in.

The S&P 500 Index was heavily concentrated in the technology sector because of the stocks' high multiples, which some indexers say is the nature of cap weighting. At the same time, the average index stock in the index was more moderately priced, and the average stock subsequently performed adequately.

RA found that, surprisingly, the bull market did not end for most companies until April 2002. The bull market that started in the early 1980s continued for two years after the tech stock bubble burst, and then the average stock joined in the decline and the entire market entered a bear phase beginning in April 2002. Six months later, the average stock started its recovery.

The cap-weighted indexes produced poorer results than the average stock in the 2001–2005 period. The market in that period favored both value stocks and small-cap stocks. The S&P 500 Equal Weighted Index had a value tilt, and value stocks drove its good returns. In the previous five-year period, 1996–2000, which was a period that favored growth stocks, the S&P 500 Index outperformed the S&P 500 Equal Weighted Index. Even so, the S&P 500 Index, with its heavy tech concentration, did not beat the equal-weighted performance by much, returning 132 percent versus 112 percent for the equal-weighted portfolio, or 2 percent a year.

Portfolio Underperformance Problems

Big companies that are respected, growing, and are known worldwide are expected to grow for a long time. RA says that if market price equals a company's fair value, plus or minus an error, the error being uncertainties relating to the unknowable future, then it is expected that some companies would have a higher market capitalization than they deserve. Those companies are overvalued.

You might look at the top ten highest-capitalized stocks today and wonder what might happen to those companies in the future. In 20 years or so, investors might look back and see that some of the top ten stocks were good companies and deserved a top ranking. What about the other companies on that list? There is a good chance that people will shake their heads and wonder what the market was thinking, that the market assigned a top ranking to some companies that were in retrospect not that good and did not deserve a high market-cap weighting. The companies with an undeserved multiple place a drag—or negative alpha—on index performance.

Investors cannot know which companies these are until after the fact. RA stresses that fundamental indexing doesn't try to pick the winning and losing stocks. RAFI doesn't make active stock bets, but simply owns a group of companies that fit its weighting methodology.

RA found that on a rolling ten-year basis, over the last 80 years, three out of ten of the top ten stocks on the market-cap rosters out-performed the average stock, and seven out of ten underperformed the average stock. An index that picks the wrong stocks seven out of ten times can cost you real money. RA considered the margin of the underperforming stocks of the top ten stocks, and it was substantial: the underperforming stocks were down an average of 26 percent to 30 percent relative to the market over the subsequent ten years.

These are only ten stocks, and because they are so few, one might wonder if their underperformances made a real difference to their index performances. It is true that they are only ten stocks, but RA found that much of the time, these stocks comprised about 25 percent of the weighting in an index. If a cap-weighted index has a fourth of its money in stocks that underperform by 26 percent or more, that index has a built-in structural performance drag.

Ways to Enhance Performance

RA studied cap weighting to see how it can be improved. Cap weighting, in its view, has a substantial growth bias. Growth companies usually have higher multiples, which means that investors think that prospects for those companies are good and are willing to pay more for each dollar of current earnings. A growth bias by itself does not hurt investors, and the companies often do grow and their high multiples are sometimes justified.

If the market is doing its job, determining worth and adjusting stock prices so that stocks sell according to their true values, those companies will be priced at just high enough multiples to justify their future growth. The returns on growth stocks will then be the same as the returns for the other stocks in the market. However, the only way an investor can earn an excess return is for these stocks to deliver better-than-expected growth.

RA says its studies have shown that cap-weighted indexes often make it certain that investors have peak exposure to a stock, a sector, or a country just before a bubble bursts. Cap-weighted index investors wind up pursuing the latest fads with high expectations and shun the stocks that are most out of favor.

One way to correct this structural problem is to weight an index equally and ignore market price, valuation multiples, and similar factors. Another way is to use the size of the fundamental factors of the companies in index calculations, which is what RA does. In its opinion, the RAFI strategies offer better liquidity, scalability, and representation of the stock market and general economy.

A company size can be measured in many ways. It can be evaluated on the amount of sales, book value, dividends, or in other ways. Weighting in these ways affects an index's returns. RA studies show that if weighting is done on any of these valuations, materially higher rates of return can be achieved on a long-term basis. This leads to the question of which measure or measures to use for valuation purposes.

RA studies suggest that no single measure leads to an ideal and complete picture of a company or group of companies. Just like a footprint in the sand has multiple measurements, such as length, width, and depth, the footprint that a company has in an economy has different aspects to measure. Using multiple measures, a composite, aggregate scale of a company in an economy can be determined.

For example, suppose that IBM comprises 4 percent of the U.S. economy as measured by dividends, and 3 percent by sales and by profits, and 2 percent by book value. An argument can be made about whether IBM is 2, 3, or 4 percent of the economy, leading to an agreement that these numbers could be averaged. The agreement is that IBM represents 3 percent of the economy and has a 3 percent weighting in the RAFI fundamental index.

The weighting doesn't have to be exactly right. All that matters is the weight be independent from over- or under-valuation, which is caused by linking weighting to the price of the stock, allowing the market price to determine the company weightings that go into the index. For RAFI, this weight is the anchor for rebalancing, and for trading against the market's constantly changing opinion about the future growth prospects for a company.

By using the fundamental type of approach, which selects, ranks, and weights companies by a company's fundamental measures, there is no linkage between portfolio weight and over- and under-valuation. RA thinks that this eliminates cap-weighting's negative alpha.

Fundamental and Capitalization Weighting in U.S. Stock Sector Weighting

The purpose of the following graphics is to show what happens in a U.S. stock cap-weighted index and a U.S. stock fundamentally weighted index over time. Look at Figure 5-1.

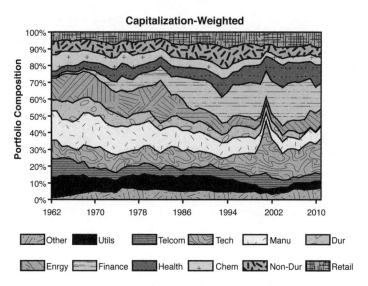

Figure 5-1 What happens with cap-weighted stocks. The index data published herein is simulated, unmanaged, and cannot be invested in directly. (Source: Research Affiliates)

RA says that Figure 5-1 shows what happens when stocks become over-valued, especially in a bubble period or an antibubble period. Each band in Figure 5-1 is a sector weighting. The most notable sector—weight bubble and burst—is the technology sector. Over time, technology had about a 10 percent weighting in the capitalization-weighted index. The technology bubble in the late 1990s saw that weight increase significantly to about 30 percent.

RA says that when an index has the most weight in the stocks that are the most over-valued simply because the prices went up, the sectors in a cap-weighted index will have peak weightings when the stocks in that sector have peak valuations. RA thinks that this is the flaw in cap weighting, that there are errors in price. Stocks move beyond fair value, in both directions, but when they become caught in a bubble, there will be more over-valued stocks in a cap-weighted index. RA says that when reversion to the mean occurs, stocks move back toward fair value, and a cap-weighted index suffers more because there is more weight in the expensive stocks. With cap-weighting, an investor rides the sectors up and then rides them down.

The RAFI Fundamentally-Weighted sector weighting, as shown in Figure 5-2, shows a different pattern than cap weighting.

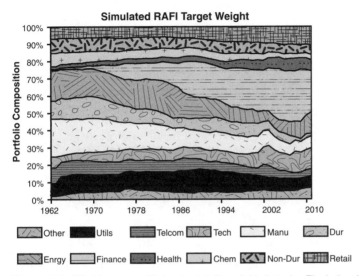

Figure 5-2 What happens with fundamentally weighted stocks. The index data published herein is simulated, unmanaged, and cannot be invested in directly. (Source: Research Affiliates)

The sector bands in Figure 5-2 are smoother and steadier over many decades compared to the sector bands in Figure 5-1. The technology sector is about 10 to 15 percent over time, and it grows slightly, which is to be expected because technology companies grow, are dynamic, and technology has become a larger factor in the U.S. economy. But investors were too excited about technology in the late 1990s and suffered a big return drag when that sector corrected. RA annually rebalances its fundamentally weighted portfolio and didn't have an overweighting in technology stocks.

Cap-weighting indexes do not rebalance, which RA says is an important difference between the two indexes. Based on research, RA says that it has shown that it has added approximately 2 percent in the U.S. index over a 60-year period, and two-thirds of that 2 percent comes from what it calls "dynamic contra-trading," which is essentially rebalancing. That is an important part because it allows fundamental indexing to capture pricing errors. If RA didn't rebalance, it says, its index would ride stocks up and down, just like cap-weighting does.

Fundamental indexing rebalances back to its "economic" anchor. RA uses fundamental economic measures because it believes it is representative of the companies in the index in relation to the U.S. economy. Equal weighting can be used, or a single factor such as dividends, or a number of other factors, but RA finds the only negative outlier is cap weighting, which uses stock prices to decide weights.

In Figure 5-2, note that the financial sector weighting has increased over time. As the percentage of profits, sales, dividends, and the book value of that sector in the U.S. economy has grown, the sector weighting in the overall economy has increased. RA says that it is not critical what the overall weight of a sector is. Over time, the fundamental index has an underweight in technology and healthcare because those companies usually have more of a "potential profit" factor. Biotech companies, for example, are "cash burn" companies and don't pay dividends because they reinvest in their growth and research, or they hope for a blockbuster drug. Tech companies often search for a new technology. RA says that when you look at the actual fundamental sizes of those businesses, they are smaller than the market expects them to develop into.

The market is sometimes right and sometimes wrong in its expectations for these growth-type companies. On average, however, RA found that the market tends to overpay for its expected earnings growth. What is important for the fundamental index is that it has a number to rebalance back to, which is the number in its fundamental weighting. RA uses trailing five-year fundamental factors, and the weightings change very slowly. The market, however, constantly changes its views on value, so when RA balances back to its fundamental weights, it doesn't matter if there are slight structural sector over-weights or structural under-weights; what matters is that the fundamental portfolio balances back to its weights and captures that change of price based on the market's expectation of the future.

Global Stock: Rolling 12-Month Average Country Weights

The differences in cap-weighting indexes and fundamentally weighted indexes also extend to global stocks, according to studies done by RA.

Figure 5-3 shows country weights in a capitalization-weighted index, and Figure 5-4 shows RA's weightings in its All World Index, which includes the U.S., developed EAFE markets, and the emerging markets. RA builds a world stock universe and every stock is compared, no matter what country the stock is in. RA fundamentally weights the 3,000 largest companies into its index, and the weights change as the fundamental scores change for each company.

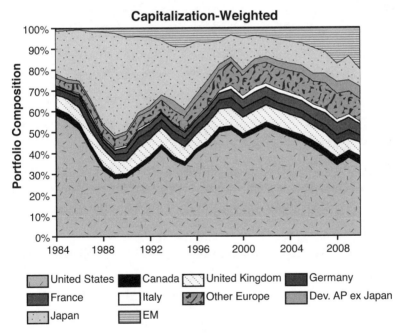

Figure 5-3 Country weights in a cap-weighted index. The index data published herein is simulated, unmanaged, and cannot be invested in directly. (Source: Research Affiliates)

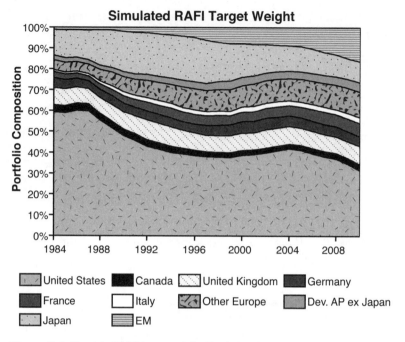

Figure 5-4 Simulated RAFI target weight. The index data published herein is simulated, unmanaged, and cannot be invested in directly. (Source: Research Affiliates)

In Figure 5-4, emerging markets, which is the top band, has gone from approximately zero percent weighting in 1984 to about 15 percent currently. This has generally followed the growth of the emerging markets' participation in the world economy. Emerging market companies have steadily grown in terms of profits, dividends, sales, and book value relative to developed-country companies, and likewise its weight in RAFI has increased smoothly, just as it occurred on an economic basis. The cap-weighted index in Figure 5-3, by comparison, grew quickly in the early-to-mid 1990s and then collapsed in the late 1990s due to several negative events in the emerging markets, such as the Asian currency crises and the Russian currency crises.

The other big story in global stocks is in the band that is second from the top, which represents Japan. In the cap-weighted index in Figure 5-3, by the late 1980s, Japan grew to be 50 percent of the world market cap. Japanese companies were expected to continue to grow, and many thought that their business models would end up taking over the world. Ten years later, in the late 1990s, they shrunk back to 10–15 percent of the world market cap. In an economic sense, Japan has been a stable part of the world's economic size at about 15 percent.

In the cap-weighted graphic shown in Figure 5-3, investors would have ridden up with the Japanese bubble and then would have ridden it back down. In the RAFI graphic shown in Figure 5-4, there was a stable band through those years and no bubble.

6

iShares

When ETFs started trading for the first time back in 1993, one of the first ETF families offered to investors was iShares. In 1996, Barclays Global Investors, which at the time was the company that owned iShares, managed the precursors of iShares, a series of World Equity Benchmark Shares referred to as WEBS. The 17 WEBS were developed by Morgan Stanley and they tracked Morgan Stanley Capital International's (MSCI) single country indices. WEBS laid the foundation for BGI's future ETF expansion. In 2000, the firm launched the brand name "iShares" by rebranding the WEBS and launching nearly 50 new iShares ETFs in one year. Over the course of a few years, iShares became the largest ETF manager in the U.S. and around the globe in terms of assets under management and number of products offered. According to BlackRock, iShares has global assets under management of more than $600 billion, with more than 460 iShares securities offered around the world.

In 2009, Barclays Global Investors and its business, including iShares, was acquired by BlackRock, which today is a leader in investment management, risk management, and advisory services for institutional and retail clients worldwide. On June 30, 2011, BlackRock's assets under management (AUM) was $3.659 trillion.

The iShares family of ETFs covers virtually all asset class exposure including sectors, regions, fixed income, and commodities. Through the iShares family, investors can customize their portfolios so that they can have exposure to fit any investment theme. BlackRock says it invests heavily to carefully manage all fund performance drivers related to its ETFs. Known as "Total Performance," the drivers include managing the fund's taxes efficiently, minimizing trading costs, and minimizing risks.

Working with well-known index providers, iShares continually designs ETFs that track indexes giving exposure to the domestic, international, fixed-income, equity, and other asset classes that investors and traders desire.

Zero-Sum Market Game

iShares ETFs replicate indexes that are mostly cap weighted, and Paul Lohrey, Managing Director and the head of iShares U.S. Product Management for BlackRock, says what the investor is pursuing is a market return with those indexes, and the market in reality is a zero-sum game. In economic and game theory, a zero-sum game is the mathematical equivalent of a situation in which a participant's gain or loss is exactly balanced by the losses or gains of the other participant or participants. If the total gains of the participants are added up, and the total losses are subtracted, they sum to zero. It is like eating a pie. A pie is only so big, and if one person takes a bigger share, there is less for the others. Eating a pie is a zero-sum undertaking, as are other endeavors in which there is only so much to go around.

Lohrey says that investing in a fund-tracking, cap-weighted index and constructing a portfolio with cap-weighted index funds means that the investor accepts that investing in the market is a zero-sum endeavor. To the extent to which an investor is investing in an index fund (for example, a total U.S. market index fund) all the fund participants in the marketplace can earn only the market's return.

He explains a zero-sum game in an illustration that imagines that there is a market containing two securities and they are both equal in size. In this example, security A earns 10 percent and security B earns 5 percent. The market, in this case, earned 7.5 percent. The owner of security A would be very happy with his purchase, and the investor who owned security B would not be nearly as happy. The owner of security B, because his security lagged the market, would research other securities and decide to trade that security. Suppose the owner of security B convinces the owner of security A to sell his shares and trade for his security B, and the same performance continued. In this case, the new owner of security A would become a winner, because he now has a winning security, and the holder of security B moves to the losing side of the trade. Suppose the market still returns 7.5 percent; well, these transactions cost something. So the holder of security A did not actually earn 10 percent—maybe more like 9.5 percent. The security B holder did not earn 5 percent either—more like 4.5 percent. So, after expenses, the market didn't earn 7.5 percent; it earned 7 percent.

Lohrey says that investors incur expenses, and some incur significant expenses, in terms of management fees, other fees, and expenses that are charged by the investment manager, as well as transaction costs. In the broader market, if you look at the total U.S. market, with its millions of investors in that market, their activity of buying and selling doesn't return a higher amount of return for the market. Lohrey says, "There is only so much economic return that the market provides over a time period. The activity of investors sending shares back and forth among each other just changes the calculus of who the winners and losers are. All that activity drags the average investor down, and the average investor gets further away from that market return because they engaged in all this activity that increased their costs. And when I say the average investor, they own half of the security A I gave in the example, and half of the security B."

Cap-Weighted Indexes Fill a Need

Lohrey says that when you invest in a cap-weighted index, you are buying the return of the market asset class you choose because you don't believe that you have the insight to know which securities will perform better than others in that asset class. You can pay higher fees to an active fund manager to select the securities that might outperform the market, but you don't have any assurance that his insights will produce a higher return after expenses and taxes than the index. So a broad cap-weighted index gives market exposure and is generally the best choice for many investors.

Cap-weighted indexes are simple. Lohrey states, "One of the hallmarks of a capitalization-weighted index fund is that there is very little trading to add or remove securities. The fund typically trades only when the index makes changes to its underlying securities, which is also not often." To get better than a market return, participants have to engage in an effort to discern which subset of securities offers a better return pattern than the market as a whole, and there is no assurance the right subset will be chosen. Alternatively weighted indexes can be used, but those that are offered as ETFs often charge a higher fee, sometimes a substantially higher fee. Also, alternatively weighted ETFs can incur additional expenses in the form of more transaction costs.

"If you think about a distribution around the market's return, hypothetically, you could broadly assume that half the market participants underperform the market and half outperform the market, because, again, it is a zero-sum game. There is only so much return that the market produces," Lohrey says. The expenses shift that distribution such that the preponderance of investors experience a return after expenses that is lower than the market's return. Lohrey says that those factors add up to an affirmative rationale that investing in cap-weighted indexes makes sense.

Weighting Other Than Cap Weighting Is Making a Bet

"Active managers make bets in their portfolios by choosing and weighting securities in an attempt to produce higher returns than the broad market, lower risk than the broad market, or both. They are trying to reflect their insights in their portfolios," Lohrey says. He believes that alternatively weighted indexes are basically the same as actively managed funds. They are purposefully constructed differently than the basic market cap approach in an effort to achieve a better result than the broad market index, such as to produce higher returns, lower risk, or both.

He says that people often confuse the rationale for pursuing a traditional, market cap-weighted investment approach and believe it implicitly relies on market efficiency. It is true that cap-weighted indexes represent the collective view of what investors believe is the fair value for all the securities contained in those indexes. In reality, the collective view of investors is almost never right. Prospectively, there are combinations of securities that yield higher returns than the market without increasing risk relative to the market. The problem for investors, he thinks, is figuring out which combination of securities produces the desired result. Proponents of alternatively weighted indexes point to the past and observe that market cap-weighted indexes have not historically produced the best combination of return and risk for investors and that there are better ways to weight (or position) stocks in a portfolio.

He says that fundamental investor proponents say that their indexes are more efficient and that maybe in hindsight, over certain periods, they were more efficient. But prospectively, the fundamental index is simply the bets made by that index maker. He says the bet for the fundamental indexer is often that small cap and value, because they are usually heavily skewed to those factors in that construction, which helps yield a more profitable portfolio. "Just like a

regular, traditional active manager puts together a portfolio, fundamental index providers believe that the indexes they've assembled,
by whatever process they assembled it, are more efficient than the
market," Lohrey says.

Lohrey believes that a well-constructed, broad, cap-weighted
index is fully representative of the publicly available stock market.
Any deviation from this, in the form of weighting indexes to reflect
a bias or a way of measuring the market, is a wrinkle that takes away
from the index truly reflecting the publicly traded market. The public
market does undergo shrinkage at times. Private equity, he says, does
at times absorb some of the publicly available companies, which takes
the companies off the market for public investors. The government,
post-2008, has also taken large portions of publicly traded companies
out of the market, therefore cutting down on the circulation of public shares. Recent government increases in regulation have prompted
some companies to go private rather than face more government
scrutiny. Some foreign companies have dropped their U.S. listings
rather than face more regulation, necessitating these companies being
dropped from some indexes.

Slicing and Dicing Cap-Weighted Indexes

Cap-weighted indexes can be sliced and diced to capture representation in whatever area of the market an investor desires, such as
regions, sectors, cap sizes, and style. Lohrey says, "Compartmental-
ization of cap-weighted indexes is one of the great features of the cap-
weighted construct. You can have different styles reflective of desired
characteristics of securities, such as you can have a value index that
reflects stocks that have appealing value characteristics, whether
you're looking at low-price-to-book ratios, low-price-to-earnings multiple, high-dividend yield, or other factors that are typical identifiers
of value. Conversely, you can construct indexes that have attractive

growth characteristics, such as stocks that have high projected earnings growth rates, and high estimated unit sales."

Lohrey says that with capitalization weighted indexes an investor also has the flexibility of investing in different capitalization size ranges, such as large-cap or small-cap, and to do this objectively. By objectively, he means that essentially, through a rules-based process, the cap-weighted indexer can identify a home for every security. Lohrey says that by slicing and dicing using different cap-weighted indexes to gain a better-than-market return, an investor makes a bet, but this bet can be quantified and controlled within a cap-weighted scheme.

Using cap-weighted indexes, an investor will have clarity regarding the degree to which he chooses in his portfolio to deviate from a purely market cap-weighted construct. In Lohrey's opinion, fundamental indexes are different in that fundamental weightings are dynamic. The factor loading of small-cap and value stocks is inherently dynamic and makes the construct change over time. This makes it hard to anticipate what direction fundamental weighting will take an investor, Lohrey believes, and an investor allows that dynamic process of weighting to allow his portfolio to drift, as the portfolio is exposed to these factor exposures over time.

Making Bets Using Asset Class Factors

As far as deciding what an investor should invest in to outperform the market, such as sectors, or cap size, or style such as growth or value, Lohrey says, "You can't isolate purely one risk factor when you're constructing bets." He makes the point that sectors have different characteristics, and "there are some sectors that have more representation in small-cap and value, and some have more representation in large-cap and growth. Financials, for example, tend to be more value-oriented, and technology tends to be more large-cap, growth companies.

"In a way, you're describing another way that in fact might be more intuitive for investors. It is intuitive for investors to think in terms of sectors, where it is hard for investors to think in terms of large-cap and small-cap. When you talk about a sector, such as technology versus healthcare versus energy, people understand, people tend to identify investments in that way."

Cap Weighting Is the Purest Form of Investing

Lohrey thinks that the purest way to invest is through cap-weighted indexes. "In that way," he says, "it's not picking a view on the market, and it's not paying someone else to take a view on the market. Investing this way is accepting what the market can deliver." This is true of cap-weighted indexes in the small-cap, mid-cap, value, growth, and other asset classes, which all have cap-weighted indexes and are replicated by ETFs.

He says that fundamental index makers do not say why they have developed their indexing methods and why their methods are better. Lohrey says that the fundamental proponents point to a cap-weighted index formula and say that cap weighting is broken, and it never produces the most efficient portfolio. Fundamental weighting advocates, in Lohrey's view, are just saying that fundamental weighting is better than cap weighting. He says, "But they don't have an affirmative thesis as to why fundamental weighting does work."

7

Rydex|SGI

Rydex|SGI is a forward-thinking asset-management firm that provides high quality, innovative investment solutions across the asset allocation spectrum, and is dedicated to meeting investors' diverse and evolving needs. The firm helps investors and investment advisors maximize the value of their investing tools and strategies, and it works at providing an outstanding level of customer service. In addition to alternative investment and index-based strategies, it offers a broad line of investment solutions, including actively managed global-, value-, growth-, and fixed-income strategies. Rydex|SGI manages assets through more than 140 mutual funds and exchange-traded products. Many of its securities have been successful and helpful, including currencies and equal-weighted ETFs.

Asset Allocation—Modern Portfolio Theory (MPT)

Anthony Davidow is the managing director and portfolio strategist of Rydex|SGI. When asked if asset allocation still makes sense for investors, Davidow says, "I continue to believe in the merits of Modern Portfolio Theory, but recognize that MPT needs to evolve. I don't think it is obsolete, but the world has certainly changed pretty dramatically over the years. Harry Markowitz and Bill Sharpe helped shape the way we invest. They taught us about the value of diversification, and how to measure risk. In 1990, Markowitz and Sharpe both won the Nobel Prize in economics for their research."

Davidow says that MPT traces its roots to Harry Markowitz. In June 1952, the 25-year-old graduate student published a paper in the *Journal of Finance* that would have a profound impact on MPT. His paper on "Portfolio Selection" received little notice at the time, but would help him win the Nobel Prize in Economics in 1990. Markowitz's paper discussed risk management through diversification. He suggested that in constructing a portfolio of two risky investments with low historical correlation, an investor could reduce the risk of the overall portfolio. Although this seems practical today, this notion of risk reduction through diversification was cutting edge at the time.

Building on Markowitz's work, Davidow says Bill Sharpe took MPT to the next level with the introduction of the Capital Asset Pricing Model (CAPM). CAPM is a model that describes the relationship between risk and expected return, which also introduced beta as a measure of market risk.

The general premise of MPT is to provide diversification advantages through investments that exhibit a low correlation to one another, which leads advisors to consider alternative investments. In periods of duress, the markets experience significant downward pressure. Davidow argues that fear and greed drive the market as opposed to underlying fundamentals.

Davidow says that after 2008, a lot of people asked, "'How come asset allocation and MPT didn't work?' I would argue that the market is more efficient over the long run, but in periods of 'shocks' to our system, it breaks down. When there are shocks to the financial markets, they don't always react in a rational way. Also, during severe shocks, the correlations among investments tend to be higher than normal. We may experience more shocks in the future, due to the inter-connectivity of the global markets."

Davidow says that after 2008, advisors are thinking differently about investing their clients' portfolios. The same old way of investing and thinking about the market doesn't work. Many advisors have become more tactical and opportunistic, and alternative investments have been deployed to dampen overall portfolio volatility.

Davidow argues that in these periods of market shocks, alternative investments weathered the storm better than traditional investments. Davidow says that much of Markowitz's work regarding MPT consisted of stocks, bonds, and cash. We live in a much more complex world today, he says, where we divide our traditional investments among large-cap and small-cap, value and growth, and developed and emerging countries. This causes investors to consider many more variables when making decisions. Davidow says, "Modern Portfolio Theory is not obsolete, but it clearly needs to evolve. With the proliferation of business news networks like CNBC, we have shortened the time frame to dissect, analyze, and respond to information. The global nature of the markets makes us more connected than ever."

Davidow thinks that the markets are set up for more shocks to the system because the flow of information is so much more rapid. He points out that European debt concerns have had a great impact on the U.S. markets. The Japanese tsunami had a ripple effect around the globe. The U.S. markets have reacted to concerns regarding Greece's potential default and potential contagion among the PIIGS (Portugal, Italy, Ireland, Greece, and Spain). "It's the *new normal*," he says, "and if you have a long-term strategy and you believe there will be shocks, you need to be equipped to deal with shocks."

Davidow says that advisors are changing the way they invest their clients' portfolios. Many advisors have taken discretion over their client accounts, so they can respond more adeptly to market changes. Advisors have also expanded their range of solutions offered to clients, and the use of alternative investments has grown to become more mainstream.

Alternative investments represent an evolutionary step, he says. Alternative investments represent a broad array of strategies, including long-short, event-driven, managed futures, private equity, commodities, and global macro among others. They typically offer different risk and return characteristics and often exhibit lower correlation to traditional investments.

Currencies as an Asset Class

Currencies represent an interesting investment option. For a long time used mostly by institutions and hedge funds, currencies represent a means of hedging international exposure and/or opportunistically taking advantage of currency fluctuations. The currency market is the largest and most liquid market in the world, with about $4 trillion in assets being traded worldwide every day. Currencies have mostly been traded by hedge funds and institutions, but have gained broader acceptance by advisors and investors.

According to Davidow, many currencies have historically exhibited low correlation to traditional asset classes such as equity and fixed income. Currencies may serve as a complement to traditional investments and may help lower a portfolio's volatility. Currencies can be used in a number of ways, such as speculating on future price movements or hedging exposure to a particular market. They can also be used to diversify cash holdings.

Rydex|SGI offers nine currency exchange traded products (ETPs) called CurrencyShares. CurrencyShares offer investors access to a broad array of currencies in a cost-effective exchange-traded structure. CurrencyShares are grantor trusts that hold foreign currency deposits in a segregated account, rather than using futures contracts or other proxies that can lead to imprecise tracking of the underlying currency. If there is interest earned from the securities, it accrues daily. After trust expenses are paid, the remaining interest is distributed to shareholders monthly. The most recent launch was a Chinese renminbi ETP.

Currencies Have Many Uses

Davidow says, "Institutions primarily use currencies to hedge their exposure. If an institution is doing business abroad, the institution can insulate the impact of currency movements and hedge with currency securities. Hedge funds use them to hedge exposure, and invest opportunistically." He gives the example of selling the euro, which has been under a lot of pressure due to Greece and allocating to the Swiss franc or the Australian (Aussie) dollar. The Swiss franc has benefitted from concerns regarding Greece contagion, and the Aussie dollar is a more natural resource and yield play.

Davidow points out that although the currency market is the largest and most liquid market in the world, it has been difficult for the average investor to invest directly in foreign currencies. Davidow says, "We have provided an exchange traded product (ET) structure, which is a more efficient way for the individual to gain exposure to the marketplace. These securities allow individual investors to gain exposure to the underlying currencies."

Not all currencies makes sense in today's environment, Davidow points out. The Aussie dollar is one that stands out as an interesting currency. The Aussie dollar is attractive due to the abundance of natural resources in Australia. They have a strong economy and have benefitted from trade with China. The Aussie dollar also provides about a 4 percent yield.

Individuals and Institutions Buy Currencies

Because Rydex|SGI actually buys currencies and places them into a bank account, CurrencyShares track the actual currency price closely, Davidow says, and "more and more, there is a lot of interest in currencies coming from advisors and individual investors. In my discussions with advisors, the light bulb goes off and people say, 'I know I need to own currencies but don't exactly know how to invest.'"

Davidow explains that for many years, hedge funds and institutions had put on the "carry-trade." He says, "The carry-trade is essentially buying the highest-yielding currency, often the Aussie dollar, and shorting the lowest-yielding currency, often the Japanese yen. But the average investor was trying to figure, 'How would I do that?' With CurrencyShares, now any investor can easily put on those trades."

An Equal-Weighted Way of Owning the Market

Rydex also offers a series of equal-weight ETFs. Davidow says that equal-weight indexes might provide better risk-adjusted results than cap-weighted indexes. He points to the S&P 500 Equal Weight Index, which has historically outperformed their market-cap-weight equivalents.

"Equal weight offers a different way of owning the market," says Davidow. "I find it fascinating that many people don't really understand what they own when they own cap-weighting strategies. Most people just accept that if they want to own 'the market,' they buy the S&P 500 Index. Nobody asked what you own and how you own it." Davidow says if you strip down the S&P 500 Index, you can see that the top ten names represent nearly 20 percent of the portfolio, and the top 50 names represent 50 percent of the portfolio.

That means that you are making a concentrated bet by buying a cap-weighted portfolio, Davidow points out and says, "If you believe that those names are the best names to own, why don't you just buy 50 names?"

Davidow says that he believes that equal weighting gives each name an equal opportunity to perform and contribute to returns over time. "What we found as we looked at our equal-weight strategy is that there are some common characteristics. Equal weighting has shown better risk-adjusted results, not surprisingly, because we diversify our risk across the portfolio." He says they are finding a true value coming from diversification and that academic research suggests there is a small-cap and mid-cap effect in that small-caps and mid-caps have delivered better results over time. With equal-cap weighting, the small- and mid-cap stocks have the same weighting as big-cap stocks, giving an equal emphasis to the smaller names.

The Value of Equal-Weight Indexes and ETFs

Rydex says that equal-weight indexes reduce the concentration risk usually associated with cap-weight indexes by not being over-concentrated in the biggest cap-weighted companies within the index. Equal-weight indexes own the same companies as the similar indexes that are cap-weighted, but each company in the index has an equal weight. Equal-weighted proponents, such as Davidow, believe this is a rational allocation of components, rather than making concentrated bets on the largest companies merely because they are larger. Davidow says, "Based on our analysis, many equal-weighted indexes retain their benefits across both cap-size indexes and geographic regions." Equal-weight sector indexes own the underlying companies equally. Equal weighting removes the impact of a few heavyweight stocks dominating the index.

To retain the integrity of equal weighting, portfolios are regularly rebalanced back to equal weights, thereby providing a more dynamic and disciplined approach. This systematic weighting approach might offer broader exposure to sources of market return and help avoid some of the problems related to concentration.

He also thinks that rebalancing, which Rydex does quarterly, is important for performance. "We see a true value in this disciplined rebalancing," Davidow says. "The disciplined rebalancing allows us to respond to changes in the market place. On a quarterly basis, we rebalance back to equal weight, trimming the companies that have appreciated, and we reallocate to those companies that have lagged. In 1998 and 1999, the markets were dominated by technology stocks; it was at the peak of the dot-com bubble. Those big tech names grew and grew until technology represented about 35 percent of the S&P 500. In 2000, the Tech Bubble burst, and we all know what happened to technology stocks."

Davidow says, "If we define 'the market' as being the cap-weighted S&P 500 Index, our results have been substantially better." He points out that since the release of the Rydex S&P 500 Equal Weight ETF (symbol RSP) in 2003, it has outperformed cap weighting by a substantial amount.

Equal-Weighted Sector ETFs

Davidow says that there has been increased interest in sector strategies. Sector strategies allow investors to over-weight their favorite sectors and under-weight those that appear overvalued. They can deconstruct the market or use sectors to complement their core exposure. Investors can choose to allocate to either cap-weighted or equal-weight sector strategies. Davidow says equal-weight sector indexes have much different exposure than cap-weighted sector ETFs.

Davidow says, "For example, many people want exposure to energy. The top five names in the cap-weighted energy index represent 60 percent of the energy sector, and the top two names represent 40 percent of the index. Do you believe that those two names represent the entire energy sector? Or, do you believe that you would be better served with broad-based exposure such as drillers, refiners, and coal and natural gas companies?"

Davidow says that when investors see where they get exposure in cap weighting they can determine whether it makes sense to invest in an equal-weighted or cap-weighted fashion. "It is startling to sit down with people and go over this," Davidow says. "People don't know they are taking on so much concentration when they are buying a cap-weighted S&P 500 Index sector."

Davidow thinks that the world is more complex today than in any time in our history. There are more investment options and a much more rapid flow of information. The basic tenets of MPT still make sense; however, MPT needs to evolve to meet the new realities. Investors need to consider a broader array of strategies and determine how to combine them to meet their long-term needs and objectives. It is both a challenging and fascinating investment world that we live in, leading investors to seek innovative strategies and solutions.

8

How Do Outstanding Money Managers Use ETFs?

ETF strategies are numerous and varied, and investors and traders use them in all kinds of imaginative ways. Some of the most innovative money managers in the industry are featured in this book, and this chapter shows you their strategies and methods. The amount managed by these professionals ranges from $10 million to several billion dollars, and their ideas and insights are clearly explained to you. Read what they say, think it over, and most of all, use their insights in your investing and trading. If you are thinking of using a money manager for all or a portion of your assets, speak with one of these contributors. These outstanding managers have been featured in top networks and publications, such as CNBC, *Barron's*, *The Wall Street Journal*, NBC, and *Research Magazine's* ETF Advisor Hall of Fame.

People can use professional money managers to help them in many ways. In the major leagues, the best and most experienced players use specialty coaches, which, to a certain extent, is what a manager is. Coaches are used in the NBA to teach experienced and talented athletes how to do things better, such as shooting foul shots and three-pointers. The top batters in major league baseball use a batting coach. Many top golfers use coaches, sometimes sparingly, sometimes constantly. If top players use a coach playing at the top levels, it makes sense that an investor or trader could use a coach. It could be that the higher the level that one is playing in, the more a player needs a coach, whether he pitches in the major leagues or trades a part of his portfolio at home.

Broadly, there are three types of investors, and for each type there are ways that a money manager can help them. The first is the *sophisticated* investor or trader; that is, one who is knowledgeable, experienced, and understands the technical aspects of fixed and equity markets. This individual or institution can use a manager as a sounding board or confidant to bounce ideas off of and to discuss potential trades. This can make the trader understand more of why he is making the trade and ensure it is a thought-out action. A trap that a successful investor can walk into is one of being supremely confident, *too* confident. Being confident is an important ingredient in being successful. But to be confident to the point of being arrogantly sure of oneself can be harmful. Having a manager to discuss positions with can be a cooling-off process and can assist in knowing more fully why you are taking a certain action.

The second investor or trader ranks under the sophisticated investor and can be considered an *experienced* investor or trader. This individual or institution has dealt in markets for years, but is not as technically knowledgeable as a sophisticated trader or has limited experience in some markets. This type of investor can be at risk because "a little knowledge can be a dangerous thing." Somewhat like hubris, this trader might think he knows more than he does, and this can lead to a costly mistake. By the way, studies show that men are more susceptible to making mistakes of hubris than women. This investor or trader uses a manager for things such as keeping up with new market trends, and there are always new trends. Also, a manager alerts an investor to new investment ideas, and we can all use another set of ears and eyes to find new ideas, because you never know when and where a new idea will emerge. With the Internet and cable television, the markets operate 24/7 and globally, and no one knows from where the next good idea will come.

The third type of investor or trader is the *novice*, someone who is not experienced or sophisticated, and has some level of experience and knowledge but is not as experienced as the traders first mentioned. The novice can use a manager for technical help, such as understanding ETF trading and how it differs from trading stocks, and other trading techniques, such as the use of stop orders.

The biggest objection to using a manager might be the cost. People say, "Why use a manager and pay them 1 to 2 percent to help when I can do it myself?" However, this is little expense if the manager adds value and helps the trader be successful. People are in the market to make real money, and a percent or two means little if one is successful. It is hard to quantify how much a manager is worth when you are figuring out a trade or an investment. To have someone on your side of the table can make the difference between good and bad trades. A percent or two is just not a lot when making decisions. The best buys are made when stocks or sectors of the market are down, and you invest against the majority view. Bearish views are needed to make a stock or ETF decline. Having someone on your side with whom you can consult is valuable in many ways, if only to reassure yourself that you know what you are doing. Some people prefer managers with large sums under management, some prefer smaller, so managers are listed by amount of assets under management (AUM).

The Best Methods for Using ETFs

On the following pages are some of the most advanced money management strategies available, and ETFs are effective in using these strategies. You can use the tools described here to achieve your objectives, and for that, you have to know your objectives. The money managers here are among the best in the industry, and their information is valuable and can be used in your investing. The more you know your objectives—the more you can identify what you are trying to do, the more you know how much risk you can stand, both financially and emotionally—the better your investment experience can be, and hopefully the more successful your investment experience. Working with an investment professional can be helpful and in the long run, it can be profitable. Use one or more professionals as you develop your investment strategies and experience.

The following disclosure is pertinent to any advice from the following money managers. They have given their time and energy to help investors understand their strategies and practices so that investors might get better returns. But there are no promises, and any investor can lose money in the market. Investing involves the risk of loss and past results are no guarantee of future returns. Any reference in these articles to specific stocks, funds, or ETFs are meant for informational purposes only and should not be considered recommendations to buy or sell. Investment choices should be made based on thorough research in light of your time frame, goals, risk tolerance, and profile.

Money Managers: How They Use ETFs in Their Investing Strategies

Every one reading this book will have different objectives and amount of investment resources. The following strategies are not that one size fits all or that each reader should do the same thing. The information is valuable in that each manager has come up with a specific strategy that helps him or her make money and/or cut down on risk. I have been exposed to these strategies and have found the ones I used valuable in investing. These managers are very well qualified and have invested and continue investing an exceptional amount of time and effort developing and refining their strategies. Some readers may be looking for a manager for their portfolio and should consider these managers. Some readers may not be looking for a manager at the present and should read these strategies to see which one or ones would be useful for him or her to use.

Path Financial

Raul Elizalde, M.S., MBA (President and CIO)

www.pathfinancial.net

Path Financial focuses on asset allocation and overall portfolio management. Path believes in using its research efforts to select and manage the right mix of asset classes while regarding big trends rather than trying to pick the right stocks. AUM $10 million.

Path Financial's Money-Management Approach

Path Financial constructs portfolios using mathematical models that are focused on achieving three objectives: diversification, periodic reallocation, and reasonable downside control. Raul Elizalde, president, CIO, and portfolio manager, says that during bull markets, broad diversification smoothes out returns, but in sharp market downturns, diversification benefits tend to vanish as all asset classes decline. Market panics elevate asset-class correlations, so diversification has to be managed properly.

Constructing a portfolio using a multiyear horizon does not work because the forecasts are difficult to make more than three months out. Path Financial builds portfolios with quarterly horizons, which is what it considers "taking small steps," to keep risks low and profit potential at a reasonably high level. As far as downside control, Path Financial believes that assets tend to follow a trend, both on the upside and on the downside, and once this trend is established, it usually continues, so prices will go further than anticipated. Because of this, Path Financial believes it is better to cut losses than to take positions and stay in them through unexpected down legs. To achieve this downside control, Path uses stop-losses when establishing positions, so that disastrous losses can be averted. Avoiding big losses is crucial to performance over the long term.

What Works for Path Financial

Path Financial offers a thorough investment-management plan to guide clients in both up and down markets by focusing on asset allocation in its management process. It believes that the best way to use its research is in selecting and managing a properly diversified asset-class mix while taking into consideration the larger market and economic trends rather than trying to beat the market by stock picking.

Investments should be attended after the initial allocations, Path believes, and it executes a plan containing diversification, portfolio construction and management, and risk controls for all market conditions. It attempts to outperform and have lower volatility than an unmanaged portfolio of stocks and bonds, and focuses on medium- and long-term goals.

Elizalde says that everything he does starts with the type of investments his client wants to have and what his client needs.

"You can break it down into two approaches: a bottom-up approach or a top-down approach," he says. "A bottom-up approach is when you start with a specific instrument, the most common example being stock picking. You start with things such as whether you like the management and you like the balance sheet, then you move on to the sector, and then you move on to the type of instrument that you're looking at."

Elizalde doesn't use the bottom-up approach and says, "That way of investing doesn't work for me. The reason is because stock picking is subject to negative surprises, and even if you can understand complex annual reports with their hundreds of pages of tables and footnotes, you don't really know what is going on, even if you have direct access to the president of the company."

Elizalde says that when an investor uses the bottom-up approach, he has to depend on detailed knowledge of companies, industries, and sectors, which is hard to do. Even if an investor understands it all, he has a finite amount of money to invest, and there are thousands of companies to analyze, so after all this studying and analyzing, an investor would have to restrict his list to maybe 10 to 30 companies to either invest in or analyze further. He thinks this approach is not a good one for most people.

He prefers the top-down approach, where he analyzes the big market and economic trends. Elizalde's decisions involve things such as whether large-cap stocks will outperform bonds or will outperform commodities, what the interest rate trends are, what the political environment is, and what the macro-economic trends are. Elizalde's background as a strategist makes it easier for him to understand the macro outlook rather than the detailed knowledge that is necessary to have when analyzing individual stocks.

Elizalde says that the Path Financial approach is unique in its use of quantitative techniques in finding the asset mix that maximizes portfolio returns with reduced risk. From this asset mix, Path constructs portfolios that can perform well with lower risk. This is different from building a portfolio containing a static mix of fixed-income and equity asset classes. Not changing the asset-class mix as market conditions dictate can cause underperformance and cause an investor to be stuck in underperforming asset classes for longer periods of time.

The asset-class allocation is the critical factor in Path Financial's portfolio strategy process. It rebalances portfolios quarterly, and uses techniques based on Modern Portfolio Theory (MPT). It uses cash as an investment asset class when it deems appropriate, for instance, to limit risk when the markets become turbulent, or to lower the correlation of its portfolios with the overall market.

Path Financial Prefers Index Investing to Stock Picking

Academic literature has demonstrated that it's far more important to get portfolio asset-allocation right than to get mired in individual stock selection, Elizalde says. If you are picking stocks, even if you get the sector right, you might end up choosing the wrong company. Say, for instance, that you like the pharmaceutical sector, Elizalde explains. The sector could do well, but what if you pick the company that gets slammed with an FDA report, one that says that its drug may have dangerous and harmful side effects? Then you would have been right on the sector pick, but not gotten paid for being right.

"Because of my top-down approach to investments," Elizalde says, "and because I like indexes, and because I like to diversify, ETFs are kind of the ideal security for me." ETFs allow Elizalde to implement a strict quantitative approach. In putting portfolios together, he looks at the history of the different indexes, determines whether the indexes are laggards or momentum leaders, and measures other factors. Then he considers which ETFs will help him the most in gaining exposure to his desired asset-class representation. When Elizalde puts together portfolios, his clients don't constrain him by dictating what he can invest in, so it is difficult to compare Path Financial's portfolios to any one index. Elizalde compares his performance of the S&P 500 Index for simplicity's sake, so he has a benchmark to judge against. Elizalde invests in a variety of indexes, and says he will not be more than 25 percent invested in the S&P 500 Index.

He says his performance should be benchmarked against cash, because he tries to avoid risk and does not heavily replicate the S&P 500 Index. What he does is generate alpha over cash by investing in asset classes according to his quantitative work to find the ones that will perform best over the next quarter. He over-weights the most promising asset class and under-weights the asset classes that, according to his processes and his opinions, do not have the highest return for the next quarter.

Path Financial is a long-only manager, meaning it does not short markets or use inverse ETFs. The universe of asset classes it considers is broad and varied. Included are U.S. stocks, which it divides into large-cap, mid-cap, small-cap, and then it divides this asset class further by considering growth and value. It also considers foreign stocks, including Developed Europe, Asia, Emerging Markets, and Latin America. On the fixed-income front, Path Financial incorporates U.S. treasuries, high-grade corporate bonds, high-yield bonds, and Treasury Inflation-Protected Securities (TIPs). On commodities, Path Financial will consider several classes, including agricultural, energy, and base metals. Path Financial will consider Real Estate Investment Trusts (REITs), and also foreign exchange.

Elizalde says that "pretty much" Path Financial stays 100 percent invested. When he takes his positions, he enters stop-losses. If any position he has established goes below a predetermined price, that position will be closed, and he uses his analysis to decide on the stop-loss price level. He says there is a trade-off between stop-loss spreads that are too wide from the market price, carrying the risk of taking a sizeable loss, and setting stop-losses tighter to the market price and limiting those losses. Setting a tighter stop-loss can incur an opportunity cost because you can be whipped out of a position by the normal volatility of the market. In his experience, each security has its own trading pattern, so some securities should be given more room to move on the downside, and stop prices will be set wider from the market price, and some securities do not need that much room, so stop prices are tighter to the market price.

What Path Financial Is Looking at for Just Three Months

The majority of Path Financial's present allocation is in the U.S. stock market, and its secondary portion is in diversified commodities. Path Financial rebalances every quarter, and Elizalde says that this rebalancing is an important part of its process. He says, "We can read the future to a certain extent. Today the 10-year Treasury Note is at 3.40 percent. We know that tomorrow it's not going to be at 6 percent. We don't know that in another year it will not be at 6 percent, but it will not be there tomorrow. In other words, as we move into the future, the determination that we know what will happen gets foggier and foggier."

The commodities that Elizalde has an interest in, subject to change next quarter, are oil and those related to food. He says that oil and food are heavily dependent on political issues, on weather, and on other things that you cannot really forecast. That is why we are seeing volatility in these commodity classes. "Many times a commodity is affected more by supply than by demand," he says, "and we learned that if there is a disruption in supply, then that will create a price disruption. That is what we are seeing happening in oil and food, because of weather conditions, because of political unrest in the Middle East and North Africa."

What Elizalde does every quarter when he rebalances client portfolios is a tactical measure. Asset relationships change over time, and he revisits allocation decisions quarterly to ensure that his positions are answering to "reality;" that is, if his tactical positions are working in the real world and if he expects them to continue to work. He thinks that looking beyond three months doesn't make sense. For him, proper portfolio management depends on being alert to changes in the behavior of asset classes, and actively managing portfolios in response to those changes. It is also important that the portfolio management process carries clear policies for action instead of merely reacting to market changes. Otherwise, the process is driven by emotions and that can be damaging to investment success. Consequently, Elizalde explains, the process requires the consistent application of mathematical and computational techniques.

Moreover, a well-designed plan to construct a portfolio that can deliver better results also can give investors a sense of control. Having control and taking steps to avoid big losses can give real peace of mind to an investor as well as provide effective portfolio management. Path Financial constructs these portfolios using short time horizons to examine and rebalance its clients' portfolios, mitigating downside risk through the use of effective trading techniques such as stop-losses, and searching for the most effective asset classes to gain alpha and manage market risk.

Oliver Capital Management

Mark K. Oliver (Founder and Portfolio Manager)

www.olivercapital.com

Oliver's first step is to gather all information about a person's financial situation, and assess goals and risk tolerance using its Comprehensive Wealth Management Questionnaire. From this, the firm makes its recommendations. AUM $80 million.

Investment Strategy

The best index is not necessarily the one that provides the highest return, according to Mark Oliver. He thinks the best index is the one that most accurately measures the performance of the style, cap size, or strategy that he wants to track. Oliver does not try to determine the index that he thinks will appreciate the most. He creates his strategy, and then searches for indexes that best fill the needs of that strategy.

The discipline and structure he learned at the elite level of sport is the same approach he uses in creating and executing strategies for his clients' investment portfolios. Referring to his Olympic pursuits in gymnastics, he says, "My coach and I would sit down every four years and put in writing a plan and strategy that we felt would give us the best chance for me to qualify for the Olympics."

Oliver says he brings a well thought-out, time-tested, disciplined, and systematic approach that he sticks to over the years, and he is not chasing the latest hot index or asset class. He plans for investment storms and knows what he is going to do before there is a storm, during the storm, and after the storm. Pre-planning for market adversity give him and his clients peace of mind. Oliver is a contrarian and regularly and systematically goes against the grain in his index and sector picks. Reverting back to his sports background, Oliver refers to what the famous hockey player Wayne Gretzky said about not skating to where the puck has been but skating to where the puck is going to be. Oliver does not buy the sector or asset classes that have been at the top but, rather, those that have underperformed and will likely move up.

Prospects and clients know what strategies Oliver follows and the cost for his services. Indexes are easy to understand, so investors do know what they are getting when Oliver manages their portfolio.

Oliver says that after working at major Wall Street wire-houses, where he had to follow the investment approach of a large firm, he is very happy to have gone independent and is free to develop his own unbiased methods. "I have about 30 years left in this business, and want to take care of my clients and be at peace with myself and what I'm bringing to my clients, so I started Oliver Capital Management," Oliver says. In constructing portfolios he often uses the iShares and Vanguard family of ETFs. His client assets are held in custody by Fidelity and Schwab, and using them frees him to purchase any securities, or choose from any ETF family. Being a fee-based advisor, he says he does not receive any added incentives, such as 12b-1 fees, "so it is truly, purely, looking for the best tools to get clients the best performance, lowering their risk, and lowering their expenses."

Oliver thinks his clients should measure him on his performance, controlling their risk, and reducing their investment fees and expenses. He uses information from the iShares.com website to help build his Strategically Engineered Portfolio Program (SEPP). The SEPP program is an asset-allocation strategy that uses indexes; these indexes are replicated by using ETF securities. Oliver uses iShares extensively, including their large-, mid-, and small-cap ETFs, and their international, emerging markets, and dividend portfolios. For special situations, he also uses ETFs. For example, Oliver added an alternative energy ETF to portfolios to get exposure to a long-term trend, thinking that over the next 10 to 20 years, alternative energy would become more a part of everyone's life on a global scale.

Oliver thinks that the beauty of indexing lies in its simplicity. Indexing is simple, and the ETF process is effective in converting indexes into easily traded securities. The seeming simplicity of matching objectives to the correct securities might have some prospects wondering if they *do* need professional help, and whether they can do the indexing by themselves. Oliver thinks that it takes more than just knowledge of the securities to be a successful ETF investor or trader, and he regards himself as the eyes, ears, and discipline for his clients because otherwise they *could* do it on their own. ETFs do not make people money because of their unique structure; they make money when they are used effectively.

Oliver tries to add value by putting a portion of clients' portfolios into undervalued ETFs. As an example, at the end of 2009, the alternative energy ETF had pulled back 69 percent and Oliver thought it was a good time to add the ETF to portfolios, which he did.

After reviewing a person's risk profile, Oliver makes suggestions about which percentage of each asset class should be owned. He recommends to each client the appropriate exposure to cap size, international markets, emerging markets, and other ETFs, as well as bond and other fixed-income ETFs. Oliver analyzes historical data to see how the different asset classes have performed and which classes gave the best return with the lowest amount of risk. From this data he determines the proper percentages of indexes to place into a portfolio in line with the investor's risk and reward profile.

Without this empirical evidence to guide the over-weighting and under-weighting of the asset classes, an investor has no choice but to guess or to simply split the asset classes evenly. Oliver concludes that this is not an effective way to beat the market.

Beating the Market

One of the problems in determining whether you are beating the market is identifying just what market it is that you are trying to beat. The media usually refers to market performance as just what the S&P 500 Index did, but Oliver thinks the market is bigger than that. He thinks performance comparisons should be expanded to include the

S&P large-cap index, mid-cap index, and small-cap index, as well as the international markets. These indexes have performed far different than the S&P 500 Index.

It is true that the S&P 500 Index, as well as other indexes, has had a negative return for the last ten years. However, the S&P small-cap and mid-cap indexes, as well as some of the international indexes, have turned in positive average annual returns for the last ten years. This performance points out the importance of having exposure to the right asset classes to outperform the market. His experience has taught him that the difference in the performance of asset classes can be significant.

Oliver thinks that one key component in beating the market is to systematically rebalance a portfolio back to its target percentages for each asset class, so that asset class weightings are optimally allocated according to empirical evidence. This rebalancing forces Oliver to systematically buy low and sell high. Oliver rebalances annually because he finds it provides the best risk-adjusted return compared to rebalancing in other time periods, such as monthly or quarterly. There are also inherent tax advantages from holding positions longer than a year.

In an attempt to outperform the indexes, each year Oliver places about 8 percent of client assets in the worst performing sector during the preceding 12-month period, such as financials, technology, or healthcare. He does this because he believes that historically the worst-performing sectors usually work their way back to the top and eventually outperform, while the top performing sectors usually work their way to the bottom.

How Oliver Capital Management Helps Clients

Mark Oliver applies skills learned in his gymnast training to customizing thoughtful financial plans for his clients. He feels that it takes discipline to stay on track to achieve financial objectives over a long period of time. His usual method is to sit down with a person and work out the person's objectives in line with his financial profile. Then he applies an appropriate and disciplined investment strategy. As part of the process, he listens to the person's thoughts, concerns, and questions. He strives to be candid and unbiased in his answers and advice.

Included in its services at Oliver Capital Management is a Comprehensive Wealth Management (CWM) system. CWM addresses issues, including retirement and education planning, asset-allocation options and models, ways to mitigate taxes, estate planning techniques, and life, disability, and long-term care insurance coverage. CWM analyzes the weaknesses in clients' overall financial plans and provides timely solutions.

As far as investing, Oliver Capital Management draws on insights and wisdom supported by MPT, and the Efficient Frontier, aiming to give clients the maximum amount of return along with the least amount of risk. After determining the optimal asset-allocation model for each client, Oliver selects the optimal percentage weighting of each index ETF to be owned. This includes allocation to large-cap, mid-cap, small-cap, fixed-income, and international ETFs, for example, as well as other strategic asset classes.

Oliver Capital Management also explores strategies to help clients and prospects reduce or defer taxes. Given the prospects for an increasing income and capital gains tax rates, Oliver helps his clients determine which ETFs are less tax-efficient and places those ETFs in tax-favorable accounts such as IRAs. Oliver believes that taxes can be one of the biggest drags on investment returns over time and built his SEPP investment strategy with a solution to help overcome this obstacle.

Using ETFs, Oliver Capital Management offers simple yet effective strategies to help mitigate capital gains taxes as well as limiting exposure to the Alternative Minimum Tax (AMT).

In addition to working with individual high-net-worth clients, Oliver Capital Management also runs retirement plans, such as 401(k)s, 403(b)s, pensions, and profit-sharing plans. The same advantages and benefits that come with investing individual clients in indexed ETFs can also be experienced by participants in employer-sponsored retirement plans. Oliver offers regular participant educational meetings and, depending on circumstances, commits to quarterly on-site visits. He feels this level of commitment is required to ensure that both the employers and employees understand the often overlooked advantages provided by investing in ETF indexes in their retirement accounts, as opposed to the traditional and less effective investment vehicles offered to participants in company-sponsored retirement plans.

Oliver Capital Management keeps its fees for wealth management services competitive. Because the firm operates on a fee-based basis and does not charge commissions, it feels it has positioned itself on the same side of the table with the client. Mark Oliver believes his primary roles as a financial advisor are threefold: to consistently and systematically apply a well thought-out, disciplined, and time-tested investment strategy using ETFs; to act as a rational sounding board for his clients' thoughts, concerns, and questions; and to be candid, forthright, unbiased, and sincere in his opinions and advice.

Metropolitan Capital Strategies, LLC

David A. Schombert (President, CIO) and Sharon Snow (CEO) www.mcsmgr.com

Metropolitan's focus is on capital appreciation and loss avoidance. MCS believes that at certain times, there are opportunities to earn good returns in broad market sectors, and only then will it invest clients' capital. AUM $100 million.

Two Portfolio Strategies

MCS focuses on the longer term and invests its portfolios to outperform from 5 to 20 years in the future. It strives to earn a 15 percent average annualized rate of return over a 5-year period. When MCS cannot identify upward moves in which it is confident of a double-digit upside return, it protects its portfolios by keeping or moving them into a low-risk asset class. It offers two investment strategies. Both are tactical strategies that use ETFs and cash equivalents to generate absolute return with the goal of returning a 15 percent annualized return over a 5-year period. The Tactical Growth Strategy utilizes options in addition to the ETF strategy to increase the cash equivalent returns. The Tactical Moderate Strategy uses the ETF strategy without options, making it appropriate for retirement accounts.

The portfolios have one of two profiles. They are fully invested in the markets with ETFs when MCS has at least a 90 percent confidence level that they can achieve at a 10 percent or greater return. The second profile is when the accounts are invested in the lowest risk asset class, often cash equivalents, due to a confidence level of less than 90 percent for achieving at least a 10 percent return in the market.

Another factor that MCS thinks is important to its strategy is the flexibility it has regarding the asset classes in which it can invest. MCS can invest in any asset class it chooses. It can invest in any market, region, sector, or capitalization. MCS feels that flexibility is one of the cornerstones to being successful in long-term investing.

MCS constructs its investment process to enable the company to make money when it believes there is low risk, and then it can protect those profits. This is called the step effect because it is analogous to climbing a staircase. The first part of this strategy is to make double-digit investment returns in a low-risk environment, which is similar to climbing stairs. The second part is to protect returns after they are made, which is similar to pausing on the landing between floors.

This process of climbing the stairs is then repeated. This investment methodology enables MCS to identify the likelihood of 10–20 percent upward market moves, giving it the opportunity to earn these double-digit percent increments. MCS believes there are 6 to 14 of these opportunities occurring in a number of broad-based indexes during rolling 5-year periods. Of these 6 to 14 opportunities, 5–8 of them carry acceptable risk, which is a confidence factor of at least 90 percent to earn a double-digit return. Only then can MCS commit its client's capital. If MCS cannot find investments that meet both the risk and return criteria, it invests in the lowest-risk asset class and augments the return with the option's strategy. Historically, the lowest risk investment class has been cash equivalents or money market funds, but in the future, it might use currencies, bonds, or commodity ETFs.

MCS Has Its Own Benchmark

"Our first motivating principle is that we are striving to achieve our benchmark," says Sharon Snow, CEO of MCS, "and that benchmark is a 15 percent annualized return over any 5-year time period. We believe investing is for the long term, and a 5-year time period is a full investment cycle." Snow says one way that MCS achieves its goal is to not lose money. Through risk-management techniques, MCS focuses on loss avoidance and capital appreciation. These two principles are paramount to making and keeping gains made in the market. MCS does not tie itself to any outside benchmark, and it has access to all global asset classes by using ETFs, and in addition, it writes options to achieve its returns. The asset classes it uses include domestic stock markets, international stock markets, emerging markets, and other markets.

Using ETFs is an important part of the MCS strategy. Snow points out that "ETFs trade all day long and they provide real-time pricing. They're liquid and fully transparent. MCS is transparent in that we manage portfolios in separately managed accounts. Clients have a third-party custodian and they can view their accounts online at any time. We have hedge fund-like results with no lock-up periods."

Being In and Out of the Market at the Right Time

MCS has an absolute return mandate so it does not compete against any stated benchmark. It can invest in any asset and it can use a wide array of ETFs for asset-class exposure. "Our universe is anything that is investable," says David Schombert, president and CIO of MCS. "We will utilize any asset class where we have low risk and a potential for a high rate of return. We consider a high rate of return to be in the double digits. We have not used all asset classes to date, but we are relatively young, fewer than 10 years old. When we reach the 10- to 15-year mark, we will probably venture into all available asset classes because opportunities present themselves usually over a 10-year cycle."

MCS believes that at certain times, there are opportunities to earn 10–20+ percent returns in broad-based segments of the market. It uses algorithms developed by Schombert that are based on technical, fundamental, and economic analysis to determine the desired asset allocation and which ETFs to use. MCS begins with charts and technical indicators looking for inflection points and/or oversold indicators. If there is an area that looks interesting, it analyzes the fundamentals for many of the constituents of the ETFs to determine whether support is broad-based. If the fundamental algorithm is positive, it can then move to the economic influences that are relevant and most likely to affect the ETF. There are 26 fundamental indicators that are the core of the MCS algorithm. The weightings of each of these indicators can be changed depending on current economic and market conditions.

"We're looking to average 15 percent per year over a 5-year period," Schombert says. "So some years we're going to have better than 15 percent and other years we may have less than 15 percent.

Basically, a bad day in our strategy is being even. What we do is wait for the risk to get extremely low and go to an investable environment. Then we go in when we know we have the potential for a double-digit return." Schombert says that in a 5-year period, MCS is in the market less than 50 percent of the time. "Generally, when we go into the market," Schombert says, "we're in there for about seven weeks to a maximum of four months, and we're pretty much back out because that's usually when the asset class that we're in has exhausted itself in terms of its potential for an upside return."

MCS Uses Dave Schombert's Algorithms to Buy and Sell

Snow says that MCS determines its confidence level when deciding to go into or out of the market by incorporating 6 technical, 26 fundamental, and 25 economic factors. MCS uses algorithms that Schombert has written, and it weighs those factors to capture the current investment environment. Every day, Schombert runs his algorithms to confirm the MCS confidence level as to whether it can get a double-digit return with low risk in the asset class it is consiering. Snow says that the algorithm gives the company a number, which has to be 90 or higher out of 100, for MCS to invest its client's capital into that asset class.

When MCS identifies an ETF whose technical profile is poised for a double-digit upward move in its opinion, it looks at the top 15 and bottom 15 stocks in each ETF. If the fundamental algorithm is positive, it moves to the relevant economic influence most likely to affect the ETF in which it has chosen to invest. It then affirms or re-weights the algorithms and runs the formula for risk assessment. If everything is positive, it decides whether to invest in the ETF, consistent with the risk rankings.

Snow says that the MCS sell discipline is the inverse of its buy discipline. The company uses technical factors so the exit signals would be that the technical indicators form a top, and the relative strength of the ETF deteriorates. Fundamentally, it can be factors, such as the end of the earnings season and all the good news is out, an economic factor, or an unexpected news announcement that is negative, which signals MCS to exit the position. Snow says, "Basically, when you have good fundamentals, such as strong revenues and earnings during a quarter, and our other factors have been met, we are typically in the market for a period of time which would correspond to a good earnings season. MCS has been mostly in broad market classes over the last five years, using broad-based ETFs such as large-cap and mid-cap, the S&P 500, the NASDAQ 100, and the emerging markets."

How the MCS Strategy Developed

Schombert says he derived his strategies from 1966 to 1982 when the markets basically went sideways. He was fascinated by reading about the few managers who actually made money in those markets and wondered what common denominators each manager had to make it possible for them to make and keep money during those difficult markets, or any market. He came up with the criteria that all the successful managers had. The first was that they avoided losing years. The winning managers were not invested in the market downturns of 1973–1974 because they were basically on the sidelines. The other similarity the winning managers shared was that they used option writing. "They didn't buy options," Schombert says, "instead, they sold options to bring in income."

The third similarity was that they shared the opinion that buy-and-hold was a losing proposition. "They called it back then, it was the first time I heard the term, a buy-and-die," Schombert recalled. "That fascinated me that buy-and-hold was a disaster. Most of the investment books that you read would say that you should buy and hold, and stick with a good company. Good companies is a relative term and all of the good companies, I found out over the course of the next 20 years after the early 1980s, was that their market prices run in cycles." Items like this have allowed Schombert to develop the indicators that he uses today in calculating algorithms to buy, sell, or hold. He says the strategy has performed as expected over the past 5 years, achieving the 15 percent gross annualized return.

Global ETF Strategies

Daniel K. Weiskopf III (Principal) and Daniel A. Faucetta (Principal) www.forefrontgroup.com

GES partnered with Forefront Capital in 2009. Global ETF Strategies provides a low-volatility tactical asset-allocation solution for individuals and traders. The global investment landscape has evolved, and as a solution, GES addresses systemic risk, diversification, liquidity, and transparency. AUM $100 million.

GES Addresses the Needs of Today's Investors

Dan Faucetta and Dan Weiskopf (the team) launched Global ETF Strategies (GES), a tactical low-volatility strategy in 2004. At that time, they were at UBS Financial Services managing discretionary accounts. As early investors in ETFs, they recognized that as an investment tool, ETFs offered the benefits of transparency, diversification, and liquidity. In addition, as portfolio managers, they strongly believed that the evolution of the ETF marketplace would help them with their systematic methodology for managing systemic risk. In 2009, they partnered with Forefront Capital to develop the firm's Exchange Traded Products (ETP) business and broaden the GES product offerings by using the team's core tactical methodology and proprietary database. GES has since added two separate global portfolio strategies structured to provide dynamic solutions for investors looking for tactical investment portfolios focused on fixed income and inflation.

GES believes its competitive advantage comes in three forms. First, as tactical investors GES manages risk in a consistent process that has been refined over the past seven years. GES defines its core asset-allocation approach according to six distinct global matrixes using a defined technical analysis methodology and a proprietary ETP database. The managers look to ETP money flows as validation of thematic trends, so ETPs are viewed both as an investment tool as well as a source of investment information. Second, GES has what it believes is a sophisticated approach by screening for differences among ETPs. The company has written a white paper on how structure matters in the ETP marketplace. Third, GES's investment process is highly sensitive to global market changes. The managers believe that by using their ETP expertise as a source of information for identifying market trends, they can allocate portfolio assets efficiently to global market changes either broadly or narrowly. This ability to adapt to change enables the managers to effectively manage risk and provide investors with the opportunity to achieve favorable risk-adjusted returns.

The GES management team believes that the ETP evolution is still in the early stages of development and expects that future product development from ETP issuers will be more complex and innovative. GES believes that its capability to generate alpha will be significantly enhanced by this progress. The development of tactical inflation strategies and fixed-income strategies are two examples of how it sees investors benefit from increased robustness in the ETP marketplace. In keeping with investors' desires for transparency, the managers write a monthly report on the industry and how their strategies are allocated. This report also includes commentary about new ETP launches, the role that ETPs can have in the 401(k) market, and global market commentary in the context of ETPs.

GES Manages Risk in an Active, Systematic Manner

The managers believe that MPT does not fully take into consideration the speed with which global economic and political changes affect correlation across asset classes. They say that MPT is less relevant today because the premise behind MPT is obsolete in that correlations between asset classes are high, not low, and therefore a diversified portfolio of asset classes cannot be expected to balance out winners and losers. Furthermore, they believe that global markets today are more interconnected and investor reactions are quicker than in the past. Therefore, traditional correlation analysis cannot match neatly or on a timely basis with risks associated in the marketplace.

However, they believe that tactical trend analysis tracks money flows and by following this, they can capitalize on efficiencies in the markets. To do this, GES developed a weekly systematic market review methodology that enables the manager to identify short- and long-term trends according to relative strength metrics and market correlations. The methodology is a top-down macro approach that ranks six different competing matrices. These matrices consist of three equity matrices, which are developed international markets, emerging markets, and the United States markets; fixed income; currencies; and commodities. As a measure of risk, each matrix includes cash as a competing risk-free investment option, which also can signal potential negative future return. The Team reviews proprietary short-term, daily pivot alerts that can signify market momentum changes over the next five to ten days. These short-term alerts are used as warning signs for risk-management purposes as well as timing for purchase or sales.

Critical to the investment process is how GES selects ETPs for investment. As the ETP market becomes increasingly complex, according to GES, buyers must examine the ingredients within the ETP wrapper. For this reason, GES believes that its capability to screen and choose the best ETPs to meet its investment objective is important to achieving its targeted investment goals. Structure matters a great deal in the ETP industry. GES has identified at least five different ETP structures and multiple index construction methodologies.

In that regard, Weiskopf wrote a white paper in 2010 entitled "ETF/ETP: Driving Alpha Through Structural Differences." Weiskopf states, "Choosing the right ETP can add as much value to a portfolio's return as choosing the right stock in a sector." As part of the investment process, the manager distinguishes different structural benefits within ETPs. For two examples, the manager looks to the process by which an ETP is rebalanced as well as the broadness of an index. These elements can be important both in evaluating an ETP's risk profile and assessing the potential outperformance or tracking error that can exist in an ETP.

Different index construction methodologies determine the concentration of index constituents in an ETP leading to material differences in performance and risk. Similarly, the team believes that portfolio construction industry exposures need to be monitored across ETPs. Credit risk is an important issue for the GES managers because Exchange Traded Notes are debt instruments. To monitor these issues, the managers use the team's proprietary ETP database in addition to outside databases and other resources that specialize in the ETP marketplace.

Adapting to Economic and Political Change

In 2004, when the managers initially launched their core strategy, there were about 170 ETPs available for investors. Weiskopf forecasts, "The number of ETPs will cross 1,400 symbolically at the same time that many U.S. equity strategists expect the S&P 500 Index value to eclipse 1,400." Faucetta says, "This forecasted robust growth makes the opportunity for GES portfolio construction to be unconstrained and the fact that our process is systematic makes our strategies highly adaptable. As more ETPs come to market, we are able to incorporate more breadth of product in our analysis and access different investment themes."

GES believes that in today's global and volatile investment world, investors need to have at least part of a portfolio allocated to an alternative asset class or strategy that can adapt to economic and political change. The GES managers believe that the combination of a defined investment process that utilizes ETP expertise to access global markets and themes provides clients with a competitive edge that is highly compelling in its capability to be dynamic in their allocations.

For example, the GES Global Core Opportunity Strategy at times might make allocations towards trends in currencies, infrastructure, inflation, and commodities. By adapting to market changes, the GES Global Core Opportunity Strategy is a long-biased strategy that strives to provide equity-like returns over a market cycle with about half the volatility. Volatility is managed by combining these alternative asset classes, managing correlation of asset classes, and at times hedging with inverse ETPs.

GES invests in asset classes as directed by the results of its tactical work, and it does not decide asset-class percentages to be invested in a traditional strategic method." "We're not extreme," Faucetta says, "We do created balanced portfolios, but if cash as an investment choice is showing greater relative performance than other asset classes, we respect the market's direction. This is what helped to defend our clients in 2008 when most all correlations went to one. The exception, of course, was cash, U.S. Treasury bonds, and gold."

Similar types of macro strategies in hedge funds often have lock-ups and are not as transparent. However, the managers believe that because transparency and liquidity are critical components for the investor's attraction to ETPs, any dilution of these features would not make sense to investors interested in a separately managed account.

As a complement to the Global Core Opportunity Strategy, GES launched two new strategies, which are Fixed Income ETFs (FI/ETFs) and Positive Return Inflation Strategy (PRIS). These two strategies are designed as an extension of the core strategy and process, but unlike the core strategy, the ETP choices have been reduced. Of the nearly 1,300 ETPs listed in the U.S., the core strategy is limited to just about 500. Based on trading volume and assets under management, the FI/ETFs portfolio is limited to 200, and the PRIS has a focus list of 150 ETPs.

GES believes that by focusing the strategy's investable universe around the objectives and correlations, investors' strategic objectives are better understood. The benefits to this fixed-income strategy is that it can target risks associated with higher interest rates by potentially being both short or long inverse ETPs, as well as targeting optimum investment time horizons on the yield curve. The expectation is that when interest rates in the U.S. begin to move up, this portfolio strategy can hedge declining values by optimizing through tactical reallocation. Furthermore, credit risk is reduced by using ETPs, which, of course, are diversified baskets of securities.

Both managers are passionate about their concerns that many retirees are locking in 2011's low interest rates and will find themselves looking at long-term losses resulting from higher trend inflation. "Fixed income at current prices," according to Faucetta, "should not be expected to be a strong total return investment class if an investor envisions higher rates in the future, and in fact, may generate negative net real returns."

Cedarwinds Investment Management

Geoffrey G. (Rip) Maclay, Jr. (Founder and Managing Partner) www.cedarwinds.com

Cedarwinds looks at the investment world from its clients' perspectives. It believes in listening carefully and doing what is right for each client. It uses a consistent, risk-based approach to help clients build and preserve wealth over time. AUM $130 million.

Cedarwinds' Core Investment Philosophy: The Strategy Is the Structure

Cedarwinds, established in 2004, is an independent, fee-only investment advisor registered with the SEC. The firm specializes in the creation and management of a comprehensive set of low-cost model portfolios comprised of structured index funds and exchange-traded funds (ETF). It believes that a structured approach to investing using a controlled blend of high-performance, low-cost, index-oriented funds represents the most effective risk-management strategy over the longer term.

Cedarwinds' philosophy includes a belief that markets are generally efficient and that price movements are uncertain. The company believes that over time, investors do not perform better than the market and that it is important to base investment decisions on facts, not speculation. It believes that facts support its view that it is impossible to consistently pick the best stocks or to identify the best money managers.

The business model has been carefully constructed to provide a comprehensive range of risk-calibrated investment solutions designed to meet the specific needs of individuals, families, entrepreneurs, retirement plans, charitable organizations, and other public and private entities.

"Rip" Maclay, founder and managing partner of Cedarwinds, says "My best advice is that all longer-term investors should be globally diversified, but in a thoughtful way." Making a distinction between diversity and diversification, Maclay emphasizes disciplined asset allocation across major global markets as a baseline strategy for managing risk. In addition to broad geographic diversification, he strongly advocates that equity holdings should be tilted more toward small and value stocks that have historically performed better than large growth stocks. Further, Maclay believes the role of fixed-income investments is crucial in terms of offsetting portfolio volatility.

In addition to its core strategy, which is a traditional buy-and-hold investment approach, Cedarwinds has also developed a short-term, tactical trading strategy that it blends with its traditional investment program. According to Maclay, "In effect, we are diversifying the time dimension with this technique."

Attempting to Lower Volatility While Keeping Upside Opportunity

Cedarwinds' focus is to help individual and institutional clients manage the risk-return relationship. In its core program, the firm has constructed a full range of model portfolios using a proprietary blend of high-performance, globally diversified, low-cost index mutual funds managed by Dimensional Fund Advisors (DFA). Through its relationship with DFA, Cedarwinds is able to provide its clients with a comprehensive range of mutual funds managed by what Maclay calls "the premiere structured index fund firm in the industry."

The global diversity of the equity holdings in its core portfolios includes positions in more than 13,000 individual companies across 44 countries. Individual investors can't buy into the DFA funds the way they could in any other fund company, but they can buy them only through a limited number of registered investment advisors, such as Cedarwinds, who have been approved by DFA to represent them in the marketplace.

In its tactical program, portfolios consist of ETFs. Maclay says, "The traditional buy-and-hold philosophy works well over longer time periods, but recent market volatility has created performance problems with this strategy, so we decided to modify our approach." Cedarwinds has blended its momentum-based program, which it reconstitutes monthly, with its traditional buy-and-hold program, in an effort to provide investors with lower downside risk while still giving investors upside opportunity.

Based on academic research and extensive financial engineering used in its asset-allocation process, the firm's investment approach is designed to provide investors the opportunity for greater portfolio returns and lower volatility compared with the results it would get with active managers. Cedarwinds advocates that its clients use the momentum-based tactical program to diversify its investment time dimension, in addition to its core program, which advocates long-term investing using a more static, global asset-class diversification strategy.

Cedarwinds Core Strategic and Target Portfolios

The Cedarwinds core investment strategy focuses on building wealth over the long run using what it believes is the most effective investment technique available to accomplish this objective—strategic asset allocation. Its roster of 13 model portfolios offers a range of risk-adjusted returns using a strategic blend of globally diversified asset classes. Cedarwinds uses a disciplined, patient investment philosophy that Maclay advocates "to avoid the seductive trap of trying to beat the market using arbitrary, short-term timing techniques, speculative stock picking or sector rotation strategies." With this approach, the fundamental objective is to determine how much risk-adjusted return each client is seeking to be consistent with individual circumstances, financial goals, investment time horizon, and risk tolerance. Cedwarwinds says that academic studies confirm that its disciplined buy-and-hold investment strategy is the most effective way to consistently capture those returns over time.

Cedarwinds says its core style makes it easier to rebalance its model portfolios and maintain a consistent asset allocation over time, and in this way, it can avoid the style drift that is often found in active portfolio management. It believes that this rebalancing ensures portfolio integrity and helps performance predictability. Depending upon each client's specific objectives, it generally employs two rebalancing techniques. First, it has the capability to automatically rebalance portfolios on a quarterly basis, which it thinks will preserve the integrity of the model portfolio baseline weighting. Its second technique is more flexible, in which it reviews underlying asset class performance at the fund level with a view to rebalance on a more periodic basis depending on tax considerations, transaction costs, and individual client needs or preferences.

Cedarwinds thinks that this approach leads to superior performance tracking and is a much easier way to track relative investment performance because its portfolio returns can be efficiently compared to similarly weighted benchmark indexes. This is in contrast to active management, where valid, long-term benchmarking might be difficult or impossible because of hybrid or blended management styles, style drifting, shifting fund objectives, fund mergers, newness of the fund, and a host of other reasons.

The investment approach used in the core strategy results in what it believes is superior compounding of investment wealth compared with actively managed funds. It concludes that this is because the company remains fully invested while also minimizing performance "leakage" because of its lower trading costs, smaller turnover expenses, and reducing its clients' capital gains taxes. In formal client presentations, the company offers examples that quantify and graphically illustrate the differences in ending investment values of its indexed approach compared to actively managed alternatives. Maclay's view is that most investors typically have little appreciation for the incredibly erosive effect that costs have on performance and portfolio values over longer time periods.

The company's core strategic portfolios address a full range of investment objectives from conservative capital preservation to aggressive growth. Its target allocation portfolios have been designed to seek superior investment returns in exchange for higher risk, using a more concentrated blend of underlying asset classes compared to its broad-based strategic portfolios. Its emphasis with both approaches has been to build a powerful set of integrated solutions enabling clients to effectively manage risk and gauge the predictability of anticipated returns.

Cedarwinds believes that its strategies are also significantly more cost-effective and tax-efficient than the active alternative due to lower portfolio turnover and reduced operating expenses. Cedarwinds believes that its approach results in more investment dollars at work, thus creating a compounding of returns that creates the opportunity for significantly higher portfolio values over longer periods of time.

Cedarwinds does not require a minimum investment to have money managed in its core program. It says fees are extremely low compared to the costs of actively managed funds or the layered costs of fund investments. Cedarwinds designs its approach to minimize taxes using low-portfolio turnover, which would result in reduced capital gains taxation. It also offers strategies to avoid short-term gains, harvest capital losses, and minimize dividend income.

Momentum-Based Strategy

In addition to the Cedarwinds' core model portfolios, it has created a tactical momentum-based strategy using ETFs to take advantage of the shorter-term dynamics in the global markets. It employs a proprietary rules-based approach in its effort to take advantage of periods when there is upside momentum in the equity markets, as well as providing downside protection when the markets are declining.

Cedarwinds' tactical portfolios are designed to take advantage of shorter-term performance momentum and market volatility that is clearly evident in the price movement of the primary global asset classes. Because these strategies involve monthly trading, this approach is much more active compared with its strategic and target-allocation portfolios. The proprietary trading strategy it has developed with this approach is entirely rules-based in its execution and includes a stop-loss provision designed to mitigate downside momentum. As a result, the company feels its program offers a highly disciplined way to take advantage of global market volatility, avoiding the typical speculative methodologies that characterize most momentum strategies.

Its tactical asset-allocation models can be used on either a standalone basis or blended together with its strategic models as a way to combine the best investment attributes of both individual approaches. It believes its tactical allocation strategy is particularly effective with tax-advantaged accounts, which are not sensitive to potential short-term capital gains taxes. These can occur due to the monthly trading activity associated with this approach.

In addition to the firm's primary focus on high quality, index-oriented fund solutions, client portfolios might also involve the ownership of actively managed mutual funds, exchange-traded funds, individual stocks, taxable or tax-exempt bonds, alternative investments, or other nondiscretionary assets. In these situations, client needs are qualified on a case-by-case basis with respect to overall account administration, portfolio composition, tax strategies, and diversification objectives as part of a total investment management relationship.

Cedarwinds says it frequently hears that the most important benefit of its program is that its clients no longer experience the anxiety associated with all the daily business headlines and latest market hype.

Longview Capital Management, LLC

Christian M. Wagner (CEO and CIO) www.longviewcptl.com

Longview's investment process involves combining relative strength with a strict sell discipline. This enables the company to properly allocate its clients' portfolios across multiple asset classes using a multiphase investment process. AUM $200 million.

Strategies to Combine Upside Potential with Downside Risk Protection

Longview Capital Management's investment philosophy is driven by a single-minded focus: to add value for its clients. This focus requires Longview to produce investment solutions that aim to consistently generate competitive risk-adjusted returns over full market cycles. It compels Longview to maintain a long-term perspective and provide innovative investment management solutions that add value for its clients. It also requires Longview to place an emphasis on risk management because understanding and managing risk are critical to

Longview's clients' investment successes. Longview firmly believes that successful investment management rests not on the ability to excel through any one of these elements, but through the combined strength of all of them.

Longview Capital Management is headquartered in Wilmington, Delaware. Longview is an independent, employee-owned company and registered investment advisor. It specializes in asset management for individuals, families, institutions, and retirement plans.

Longview concentrates on tactical asset management; its investment process incorporates fundamental and technical analysis. It is active when it comes to asset management, having the capability to quickly move fully into any asset class, including cash, and employ a strict sell discipline to limit downside risk. According to Christian Wagner, CEO and CIO, "We have entered a new era in the global marketplace, characterized by rapid, dramatic, and turbulent changes. Quick response is paramount."

Longview's investment process starts and ends with risk management. Wagner points out, "Our overall goal is to win by not losing; we have a flexible investment mandate, focusing on capital appreciation when the markets are performing well and capital preservation when they are not."

Longview's Global Allocation Fund: A Flexible Strategy for a Changing World

Longview recently launched the Longview Global Allocation Fund (symbol LONGX), which is structured to seek opportunity using any asset class, any sector, any market cap, anywhere in the world. The Longview Global Allocation Fund seeks to preserve and grow capital by producing absolute returns with reduced volatility. Longview believes the changing global landscape presents investors with an unprecedented opportunity to shift its investment perspective, establishing a global allocation strategy as the core of its investment portfolio. The Longview Global Allocation Fund attempts to help clients achieve their long-term financial goals by providing an actively managed strategy, a tactical approach, downside protection, and a highly experienced management team.

The fund is actively managed, and the investment process is driven by a mix of fundamental and technical analysis, with an emphasis on relative strength. Longview seeks to identify fundamental trends and changes in the economic environment. Longview's investment process allows it to be properly allocated across multiple asset classes, sectors, capitalizations, and styles. Longview's investment mandate allows it to change the construction of the Longview Global Allocation Fund at any time, based on the changing realities in the global markets. Wagner says, "We use the full scope of the firm's resources to uncover opportunities anywhere in the world, whether they're in stocks and bonds, or commodities and currencies."

Downside Protection

In this uncertain world, Longview recognizes the need to overweight, under-weight, or simply avoid specific areas of the market based on the environment. Longview does this to achieve excess returns or to avoid excess volatility.

Longview employs a strict sell discipline with the goal of minimizing risk and maximizing capital preservation. The Longview Global Allocation Fund is diversified across markets, classes, sectors, and styles with the goal to produce absolute returns with reduced volatility. In addition, the Fund will also attempt to hedge against extreme market outcomes. Wagner states that, "Longview's disciplined, objective, model-driven approach removes emotion from the investment-decision process."

Longview Offers Several Strategies

Wagner says that the kind of strategy that Longview has constructed, a global-allocation strategy, is needed by investors. He says, "We have found that most investors have not embraced true global investing, and many end up—if they're being aggressive—with 5 to 10 percent of their portfolio in international equities. Five to 10 percent is not nearly enough in a true global-allocation strategy."

Wagner says that Longview's strategy focuses on seven separate asset classes, which are U.S. equities, international equities, domestic debt, international debt, commodities, currencies, and what they term occasionally as the most important asset class, cash. "What we do," Wagner says, "is over-weight those asset classes that are showing the greatest amount of strength. By doing that we are able to position our clients to benefit from the majority of the upside, while sheltering them from the majority of the downside."

Longview manages six separate models across multiple asset classes, including commodities, currencies, and fixed-income portfolios. "And then, based on our research, we will over-weight or under-weight or not weight at all those models within our fund." Although Longview does have some institutional clients who use the six model strategies, most of Longview's clients are invested in the Longview Global Allocation Strategy. Wagner says this is because the strategy provides market-like returns with lower risk, lower beta, and lower volatility, which is what Longview's clients are looking for.

All of Longview's strategies run simultaneously and then Longview decides, based on research, how to apportion investment capital. "We might decide," Wagner says, "that based on our research we're going to position 33 percent of the portfolio in domestic equities, 30 percent of the portfolio in commodities, and position the rest in cash." Wagner says a client ultimately ends up with a globally diversified portfolio, "which is not only diversified by asset classes, but is diversified in the sense that securities are coming in and out of that portfolio as they hit certain price targets or stops."

What Longview hates to do more than anything, Wagner states, is "give money back." In certain markets, Wagner says it may take a step back and deem that the market is too volatile, it is not comfortable with the risk-reward ratio, and at that point it will increase its cash position. "If we miss a market," he states, "then we've missed an opportunity. In today's investment world, there seem to be new opportunities fairly frequently. The buy-and-hold markets that we grew accustomed to—they simply are no longer around." Wagner gives an example of how conditions have changed in the stock market. "Today's electronic markets have turned the floor of the NYSE into a media stage. Ten years ago it was very difficult to conduct an interview from the floor."

Longview Selects from Many Asset Classes, Including Alternatively Weighted Indexes

Wagner says that Longview is now focused on U.S. equities and emerging markets, specifically certain sectors. He currently likes healthcare, industrials, raw materials, and utilities. He likes utilities because they are defensive in nature when things tend to be volatile, and they also pay a good dividend. He says, "When was the last time someone went out and started a brand new utility—it doesn't happen. Our feeling is that the large utility companies must acquire smaller utility companies because there is no organic growth in the space." He likes utilities located in the U.S., developed international countries, and emerging markets.

The Longview strategy to weight a portfolio is to take less risk and still deliver market-like returns. This includes the weighting of indexes, and it considers weighting such as cap-weighted, equal-weighted, revenue-weighted, and earnings-weighted. The weighting decision is based on its opinion of where they are in the economic cycle.

"If we look at the S&P 500, we see that the top ten holdings make up more than 20 percent of all of the assets in that index. The top ten, then, take up a pretty large block. That's not a bad way to be positioned if the markets are very defensive," Wagner says. "Conversely, if the economy is in an early stage economic cycle, the best way to benefit is in the small- to mid-cap space, those companies that are growing at much more rapid pace than the large-cap companies." The returns on the equal-weighted S&P 500 "are staggering," Wagner says, compared to the returns on the cap-weighted S&P 500. He says since inception, the S&P 500 equal-weighted ETF is more than twice as good as the cap-weighted index. Wagner says, "That most investors and for that matter most investment professionals have no idea that they can invest in the S&P 500 Index on an equal-weighted basis is one of the best kept secrets in the industry."

Wagner says that at times, a cap-weighted ETF is preferable to an equal-weighted ETF. "Generally that time frame when we prefer a cap-weighted index is in a late-stage economic cycle. The last time we saw a cap-weighted index come into favor was late 2007," he says. "And that was really a more defensive market, a late-stage market. People started to position themselves into more defensive sectors, such as consumer staples, utilities, and sectors such as that." Wagner says that Longview looks at that stage of cycles from an economic and market-timing perspective, as well as a cycle-timing perspective.

Wagner says that after avoiding the market implosion in 2008, Longview was early to go for long domestic equities, specifically the technology sector, in March 2009. It implemented many strategies that would benefit from not only the emerging economy, but how these companies could compete in the global economy. One of the cheapest ways for companies to compete, Wagner decided, was to use technology. It was cheaper for companies to invest in technology than to hire new workers. "We've seen that time and time again," Wagner says. "So we began to invest in equal-weighted technology securities." This strategy worked out well for Longview's clients. "We delivered a lower beta strategy with above-market returns at that time," Wagner recalls.

Deciding on what investment strategy to use depends on how an investor looks at the market, Wagner says. "We found that a lot of investors are looking at the market in too short of a cycle. The way we look at things is that we lengthen the cycle for a certain portion of the portfolio and make that our core portfolio. And then we shorten the cycle in some other areas, because there is going to be a lot of market volatility." Wagner says volatility is high in the commodity markets, especially silver and gold. Shortening the cycle on part of the portfolio has enabled Longview to deliver positive returns on a non-correlated basis.

Efficient Market Advisors, LLC

Herb W. Morgan, CEO, Chief Investment Officer
www.etfaccount.com

Efficient Market's 15 portfolios have been constructed by combining MPT with tactical and opportunistic overlays. The base MPT portfolios are constructed using financial modeling software. AUM $200 million.

Efficient Market Advisors Combine Modern Portfolio Theory with Real-World Tactical Decision and Opportunistic Bets

Efficient Market Advisors (EMA) constructs portfolios using its interpretation of MPT, and utilizes sophisticated financial software for its modeling to pick the most promising asset classes for each portfolio. EMA then assigns each client to a model based on the client's answers to a propriety risk profile and time horizon questionnaire. According to EMA, MPT believes that at every level of risk an investor takes, there is an optimal asset allocation that is expected to produce the highest result. EMA determines the broad asset class ranges by a complex mathematical technique known as optimization.

Optimization is known for being used in mathematics and computer science to generally extract the best elements from sets of optional alternatives. Optimizing solves problems by minimizing or maximizing the value of variables. In portfolio management, optimization is used to create efficient portfolios that emphasize the asset-class weights that are the most promising given an investor's stated time horizon and willingness to accept volatility.

Clients of EMA include individual investors, whose assets are held in separate accounts, and financial advisors who hire EMA on behalf of individual investors. In separate accounts, the assets are held in the client's name at an independent non-affiliated custodian, and all transactions are reported to the customer. EMA has constructed 15 portfolios using MPT. The asset classes used are large-cap stocks, mid-cap stocks, small-cap stocks, large-cap international stocks, emerging market stocks, intermediate-term, investment-grade taxable bonds, short-term U.S. government bonds, real estate, commodities, REITs, diversified alternatives, emerging market bonds, and cash.

The Roots of Efficient Market Strategies

To make money in the market you have to buy low and sell high, and EMA attempts to do this both through its tactical investment decisions and also by rebalancing its portfolios on a regular basis. Rebalancing is the practice of keeping targeted asset-class allocations constant by consistently and methodically selling portions of an asset class when that asset class has grown to be a larger percentage of its target allocation. EMA believes in studies that show that periodically rebalancing portfolios between different asset classes, such as bonds, stocks, and cash, can reduce overall risk. Not only can rebalancing lower risk, but it can increase return over time.

The investment philosophy of EMA is rooted in academic studies, which are used to construct its base strategic asset-allocation models. It also subscribes to the Efficient Market Hypothesis that proposes that the market price of a security incorporates all the known information about the security, and that no investor knows more than any other investor about the future price of the security. To implement this belief, EMA utilizes low-cost, exchange-traded funds to represent each asset class in the portfolio. EMA believes that the vast majority of an investor's total return is determined by its asset-allocation decision. For this reason, EMA focuses its research on asset allocation exclusively.

EMA uses ETFs for many reasons. It prefers lower-cost, large, and more liquid ETFs. It likes ETFs over traditional open-end mutual funds because ETFs deliver many high-tax efficiencies, and EMA believes its clients will have little or no annual capital gains distributions from the funds themselves. This gives EMA greater control over the capital gains taxes its investors pay. It also reviews accounts annually to find swap opportunities, which is also known as tax-loss harvesting. Tax-loss harvesting occurs when a client has a loss in a position, and the loss position can be sold and the position swapped into a similar ETF, so that the asset-class exposure is kept open. One example given by EMA is selling the iShares Russell 2000 small-cap ETF (symbol IWM) after a market decline and replacing it with the iShares S&P small-cap ETF (symbol IJT).

Herb W. Morgan, CEO and CIO, says that EMA approaches the way it handles accounts from the perspective of how it can help clients using its investment philosophy, and thinks that the separate account structure while using ETFs is a natural evolution. The separate account structure for individuals was set up in the mid-1970s when E.F. Hutton, a long-gone brokerage firm, started a consulting group that began to offer managed accounts to individual clients for the first time. The market since that time has grown massively, but Morgan says the separate account market "has failed to deliver the right thing at the right price to the right people. This is because while we have given the average investor access to, say, an international large-cap manager, or a high-yield bond manager, we haven't given them proper asset allocation. The average separate-account client account holds about $750,000. The average client has three managers. Therefore, clients have three asset classes with one manager in each asset class." Morgan thinks this is not proper diversification and puts clients in an unreasonable risk position.

ETFs Perfectly Fit the Separate Account Model

Before Morgan started EMA, he ran the managed account business of a major broker dealer. It frustrated him that his team would educate financial advisors on the importance of asset allocation but didn't have a tool with which the advisors could implement true asset allocation in separate accounts. This made it impossible for advisors to cover all the asset classes. Morgan says that in addition, there was risk by having only one manager per asset class. If the manager was out of style or made investment mistakes, the portfolio would not have exposure to the asset class. Trying to fit an asset-class exposure with securities that didn't quite cover the exposure would be like trying to fit a square peg into a round hole.

Using ETFs for separate accounts was a natural evolution. Morgan says, "You get all the benefits, that is, individual cost basis, you own your own securities, you're not at the whim of people redeeming and causing you to have capital gains. You also now have the ability for the average investor, who has a $750,000 portfolio, to actually cover every asset class and get institutional-caliber asset allocation, such that their managed account now can mimic and mirror for the first time what a large pension plan, a large foundation, or an endowment gets, when those institutions work with a traditional pension consultant."

Morgan says that EMA takes the asset allocation concept and applies it to the way it manages money. EMA calls its investment philosophy "The Three-Legged Stool," and combines strategic asset allocation with tactical asset allocation, and combines these factors with opportunistic movements in the portfolio. For strategic asset allocation, EMA analyzes the historic return of asset classes and their inter-relationship to each other, and then runs simple regression techniques using the aforementioned modeling software. From this, EMA comes up with strategic asset allocation models based on an investor's time horizon and risk tolerance.

EMA Takes Strategic Allocation Further

Morgan says strategic allocation is a reasonable place to start, but it's not reasonable to stop there, and this is the difference between EMA and other strategic asset allocation managers. He says some other strategic allocation managers argue that a manager should use only data and never use opinion or economic analysis to make adjustments on a tactical basis. Using such things as opinion is a futile endeavor, the other managers' argument goes, and that you should simply do a strategic allocation rebalance once a year and be done with it.

Morgan finds this strategy limiting, saying, "Strategic asset allocation is very limited from a statistical basis because you don't have the minimum number of data points from which you can draw conclusions. Statistical relevance is achieved only at 100 data points or more, and we simply do not have 100 years of index data on anything, with the exception of the Dow, and that it not enough."

The other problem, Morgan says, is that you can't have *"ceteris paribus."* *Ceteris paribus* is Latin and translates roughly into "all other things being held constant," or "all other things being equal." All things are not always equal in the stock market, and factors are always changing, so it is almost impossible to compare different market data absolutely. Morgan says, "To analyze data, let's say that it is the Dow, as an example, comparing it to T-bills, which is a two-asset class world. You must have *ceteris paribus*, that is, everything must be constant in the world. And we don't have the ability to do that statistically with the Dow. In other words, we'd have to go back and adjust every year of the Dow for changes in tax laws, for pre-Enron and post-Enron conditions, pre-backdated option scandals and post-backdated option scandal conditions. So it's really not reasonable to manage money only on a purely strategic basis."

Morgan thinks, however, that strategic allocation is a great place to start. He says the best way to proceed is to develop strategic models for clients with a number of investment horizons, such as 10-year, 15-year, and 20-year time frames. The second part is tactical asset-allocation modeling. Morgan says at this point, "We ask where are we on the economic cycle? What do we believe based on our macro-economic and fundamental analysis? We are fundamentalists as opposed to quants. Actually, we start quant and go fundamental. We under-weight and over-weight each asset class based on our economic view of the world, our political view, our interest rate view, and other factors." Those are what Morgan calls "proper tactical adjustments," and says he is not comfortable making large tactical bets. Other managers, he adds, might have strategies that tell them to leverage in or out of the market. He doesn't think that this type of investing is consistent with the investment duty that he has toward his clients.

The third part of his overall asset allocation model is "opportunistic." "Opportunistic to us," Morgan says, "is things that occur in the course of a calendar year that we never thought of or predicted in our view of the world, which we adjust regularly." He says that a great example of unimagined occurrences happened in the summer of 2008, when oil hit $143 a barrel. Morgan says, "On that day, Goldman Sachs came out with a report that oil was going to $300 a barrel, and the peak-oil theorists were all over the news, getting all the headlines at the time. We said that this was something that we never predicted would happen, and let's completely sell out of our commodities position. We did that, it turned out to be a very prescient decision, but that was opportunistic. We never predicted oil would be so overvalued."

Morgan says that opportunistic bets are conditions that you have to be willing to react to when they present themselves, but you didn't think of them or plan for them; rather, they appeared and a portfolio manager must be willing to move quickly.

Smart Portfolios, LLC

Bryce James (Founder and CEO) www.smartportfolios.com

Smart Portfolios assesses risk against reward in constructing portfolios. It maintains that standard statistical methods do not accurately convey the frequency and magnitude of extreme financial events. Smart's advanced risk technology is structured to better optimize risk-adjusted returns. AUM $225 million.

Smart Portfolios Improves Risk Analysis and Portfolio Optimization

Bryce James, founder and CEO of Smart Portfolios, has developed a state-of-art asset allocation system called Dynamic Portfolio Optimization (DPO). The DPO model applies a methodology called Extreme Value Theory with other advanced solutions to estimate the risk-adjusted returns of competing investment opportunities in an effort to better optimize a portfolio's asset mix. Smart Portfolios uses what it believes is a superior method for understanding risk in its effort to enable better allocation decisions to result in higher risk-adjusted portfolio returns. Its DPO model also incorporates an advanced diversification model to measure changes in correlation during volatile markets, which it says further reduces the odds of large losses.

Smart Portfolios believes that the upgraded asset allocation elements in DPO make DPO the most advanced asset allocation solution available. Smart Portfolios applies DPO to portfolios of mutual funds and ETFs. These optimized portfolios are available through investment firms that hire Smart Portfolios as a sub-advisor, an overlay strategy, or as a separately managed account. Smart Portfolios also manages a mutual fund as a sub-advisor to a mutual fund family, and provides overlay management inside the variable annuity and variable life insurance products of several large insurance companies.

Its goal is to create investor portfolios that dynamically adjust the risk tolerances, return expectations, and correlation estimates of investments as markets change, thereby maximizing the risk-adjusted returns for investors and reducing the odds of large losses.

Asset Allocation Models Are Not Meant to Be the Same, Although Most Are

James says that in the 1950s, Harry Markowitz created MPT to manage investment portfolios, and that MPT states that if assets are diversified, the investor will get better returns and less risk. He says that the implementation of MPT is performed with a method called Mean-Variance Optimization (MVO), which uses historical data to calculate the returns, risk, and correlation of securities. Using a three-step approach, one can calculate the optimal portfolio mix on the efficient frontier to maximize risk-adjusted returns. Because MPT/MVO relies entirely on the average of historical prices, the average calculation of risk, return, and correlation is slow to change with new data. He adds, "It's like throwing a bucket of water into Lake Michigan."

He says this is how you determine the recommended asset mix of 60 percent equities and 40 percent bonds. MPT/MVO takes the average risk and return of each asset class (typically the S&P 500 for stocks and the Barclays Aggregate Bond Index for bonds) and uses the historical correlation between them to determine the optimal mix on the efficient frontier. James says, "This is also why so many financial advisors tell you to buy and hold, because new information gets severely diluted." He says what makes MPT/MVO less robust is that it uses the average of past performance to predict future results, even though Wall Street marketing material clearly states that "past performance is no guarantee of future results."

According to James, in 1976, Roll and Ross from the University of Chicago realized that economic cycles affected security prices. In their research, they took the long-term, asset-allocation model mix recommended by the MVO model and tilted it to a more bullish or bearish state depending on the economic forecast. If they thought that the market would be in a good economic period, they would change the asset-allocation mix more towards equities. For example, they would weight 70 percent equity and 30 percent bonds instead of the more common mix of 60 percent equity and 40 percent bonds. Conversely, if they thought bad economic times were coming they might allocate 50 percent equity and 50 percent bonds.

The concept of using economic data (econometrics) to tilt the asset mix is called Arbitrage Pricing Theory (APT), according to James. He says that the most advanced model following APT is the Black-Litterman model, released in 1994. James points out that there are more than 100 economic indicators to choose from when making an asset-allocation decision using APT. An investor has to know which ones to use and how much to weight them. There is also the question of which economist to follow, making things complex with an inherently large risk for errors.

In 2005, Smart Portfolios released its DPO model, which uses current market activity to forecast the optimal portfolio mix. James says that understanding the importance of current market data is critical in properly analyzing risk, returns, and correlations, determining the true optimal asset mixes on the efficient frontier. James says, "Current information is far more valuable than the average price of the previous 40 years. The DPO model utilizes the historical averages as a placeholder, but implements advanced mathematics to guide current allocation decisions."

James says that the buy-and-hold strategy is less effective because markets go through economic cycles, as recognized by Roll and Ross. There are many studies showing asset class performance, but James says the most important factor in modeling is in selecting the correct time series to be analyzed, and in knowing how to properly weight that time series. If a shorter time series is used, its return forecast cannot be assumed to be indicative of a longer time series forecast. James says many studies show that over the long term, equities return 9 percent per annum. But a 15-year time series ending in 2000 would have estimated a 17% return forecast. A ten-year forecast ending in 2010 would show a negative return for the S&P 500 Index. Many studies now show that equities will return 3 to 4 percent annually in the future, as markets have declined during the past decade. "That is because they are looking in the rearview mirror and they don't know what time series to use," James says, referring to market studies.

James says traditional asset-allocation models act like a *Farmers' Almanac*, and they rely on using the mean-average return of a selected time series, normally 38 years, to capture a full market cycle, to predict future results, and specifically return, risk, and correlation. Again, this is how they arrive at the commonly recommended allocation mix of 60 percent equity and 40 percent bonds. James says that asset allocation return is different for most decades. In studies used by Smart Portfolios, in the years 1960–2010, equities generated higher returns with higher risk, whereas bonds delivered lower returns with lower risk over that 50-year period. As we are taught, more risk, more return. But looking at the efficient frontier for the optimal mix by decade, you would see that you would have been much better off being in bonds in the decade of 2000–2010. Bonds produced more return with less risk, contrary to popular belief, and the efficient frontier was actually upside down, as riskier investments delivered less return.

The problem in asset-allocation modeling lies within the mean-variance construct, James says. How can the average return of 40 years possibly be an accurate indication of current market risks or likely return results? That is, unless you have a 40-year investment horizon. Using an advanced asset-allocation model, an investor is even better off rebalancing monthly, instead of by the year as most portfolio investment models do. Smart Portfolios builds real-time, efficient frontier models, which dynamically adjust for current market conditions. James says this is akin to a Doppler radar approach to investing versus the traditional Farmers' Almanac method of mean-variance.

James says that Wall Street spends billions each year on research, market timing, transaction costs, and other fees, and little, if any, on asset-allocation research. Yet many studies, such as the Brinson, Beebower, and Singer study (Gary P. Brinson, Brian D. Singer, and Gilbert L. Beebower, "Determinants of Portfolio Performance II: An Update," *The Financial Analysts Journal*, 47, 3 [1991]) demonstrate that 91.5% of the quarterly variation in returns is due to asset allocation.

As far as asset-allocation research, James says, "Few know how an asset-allocation model actually works, or what makes one model different from another, or how to improve the performance of the models. That's what we do." James says that Wall Street loves to cite that its asset-allocation model is based on the Nobel Prize-winning concepts of Harry Markowitz, who earned his prize for his contribution to finance from his work in the 1950s. Meanwhile, James says, we have Nobel-winning laureates from this decade, specifically Granger and Engle, who actually won their prizes for managing a timeseries similar to the Doppler effect. "Wall Street is stuck in an old paradigm," James says.

James says Smart Portfolios combines the use of non-normal distributions to better predict extreme events, with the works of Granger and Engle's math, known as Generalized Auto-Regressive Heteroskedacity (GARCH), to better predict current risk, return, and correlation, thereby creating a better asset-allocation mix to seek superior risk-adjusted returns.

What Creates Changes in Securities Prices?

James says you should have an investment philosophy, methodology, and strategy before you make an investment. His theory is that all investors make the market to some degree, and this includes hedge funds, mutual funds, high-frequency traders, 100-share traders, and anybody else who buys and sells securities. He says that markets are driven by participant expectations. For example, that 100-share trader might think that Google will earn a certain number, a mutual fund might think that interest rates will spike up, a hedge fund may believe that the market is going to crash, and all this goes into making a market and the resulting shape of a security's frequency distribution; so the shape defines the security.

"Price changes all fall under four basic premises," James says, "it's one or more of the following: fundamental, technical, economic, or perhaps sentiment, which is behavioral. Under each of those premises would be sub-categories; such as if it is fundamental, it might be P/Es, growth rates, price-to-book, price-to-cash flow, or dividend yield." If an expectation changes, James says, the price of an asset class will change, and often dramatically, and so will the shape of a security's price distribution. A report by Bianco Research, LLC ("Are Long-Term Earnings Projections Getting Worse?" by James Biano, April 29, 2011, *The Big Picture*, http://www.ritholtz.com/blog) found analysts' 12-month earnings forecasts from one year prior were off by more than 50 percent in 2010 when compared to the actual 12-month trailing operating earnings results. "Wall Street is full of bad data and bad estimates," James says.

What is notable about changes in security prices, especially during market bubbles, is that the shape of a security's price distribution changes as well. They become skewed to the left in bear markets and skewed to the right in bull markets. Also, no security has a normal distribution. Distributions have "fat-tails" caused by extreme events, or alternatively known as "outliers." James says that "outliers are the norm, not the exception." James says Smart Portfolios uses a scientific process and newer mathematics to estimate risk, to forecast returns, and diversify assets. James says "The less you lose, the less you need to earn to get better performance—we want to know our risks!"

Monument Wealth Management

David B. Armstrong, CFA, Managing Director

www.monumentwealthmanagement.com

Monument Wealth Management (MWM) offers an asset-management strategy that alleviates the need for its clients to worry about daily market changes. Its clients are free to concentrate on short- and long-term goals. MWM monitors and updates portfolio performance continually. AUM $250 million.

Monument Wealth Management Structures Portfolios for Varied Client Needs

MWM is comprised of a team of financial advisors who have more than 50 years of combined experience helping clients meet objectives and investment goals. These clients include wealthy individuals, corporate executives, business owners, and other investors who want to benefit from the sophisticated financial planning, portfolio management, and personalized client services. MWM is an independent, wealth-management firm that provides unbiased financial advice that is tailored to clients' individual situations and desires. Each MWM partner has a financial specialty, which allows him or her to provide focused advice for every dimension of the clients' financial lives. Its tag line "We believe in being different" drives not only the Private Wealth Planning and asset-management strategies, but also the firm's culture.

MWM believes that no matter how much capital high-net worth individuals and families have accumulated, they probably have anxiety regarding their assets being depleted and face considerable challenges in preserving and distributing wealth. MWM's Private Wealth Planning process is designed to alleviate that anxiety and help ensure that daily income needs are available no matter what the markets are doing. MWM helps its clients determine what their needs and aspirations are, and it attempts to match portfolios to match these needs.

Also important is that its clients' long-term goals and legacy wishes are funded, and portfolios are built in an attempt to meet these goals.

MWM offers its Private Wealth Planning services to all investors without the requirement that MWM manages the assets. Private Wealth Planning clients can take the plan designed for them by MWM to any asset manager for implementation. The MWM Private Wealth Planning process will clearly define a client's survival needs, as well as lifestyle goals and legacy aspirations. MWM's approach to investment management is grounded in three principles, which are low cost, tax efficiency, and effective diversification. When clients choose MWM to help invest their assets, they often elect to have MWM manage their portfolios on a discretionary basis, which means that MWM will make investment decisions on their behalf.

MWM offers two types of strategies. The first is its core portfolio strategies, which are developed to include any special income needs. These portfolios, which consist of the bulk of any client's assets, are long-term, well-diversified strategies, have a low amount of turnover, and are low-cost and tax-efficient. The second are satellite portfolio strategies. These portfolios are more tactical in nature and are designed to capitalize on current or shorter-term market conditions with less consideration given to tax efficiency and overall cost.

Learning How to Manage Money

David B. Armstrong, CFA, Managing Director, and one of the founders of MWM, says that after college he became an officer in the U.S. Marine Corps. After spending seven years on active duty, which included a combat tour in Mogadishu, Somalia, as well as multiple other deployments to the Middle East and other places around the world, he started investing his own money, which he had saved up because he had no place to spend it while he was being deployed. He bought books on mutual funds and started reading everything he could on asset allocation and money management. He says, "It kind of became my hobby, and what started out as my hobby became my passion."

Armstrong went to graduate school and received an MBA, and then became a Chartered Financial Analyst charterholder because, he says, "I wanted to learn every single thing I could about investing money." After working for a major brokerage firm, he learned that in addition to managing money, he wanted to run his own business. On top of wanting to be an entrepreneur, he found that managing money under the independent platform eliminated a slew of conflicts of interest between himself and his clients. Armstrong and his three other partners started MWM in May 2008.

Armstrong says that by the time they started MWM, he had learned many lessons about how to manage money, and told of his early days when he was working for a brokerage firm. When he worked for the brokerage firm, he did what most wealth managers did, which is to take the position that instead of managing the money he would give it to the experts to handle, meaning he would outsource the money to outside third-party professional managers. He was a wealth manager, but his function was as a relationship manager, and he was expected to manage the relationship.

Armstrong says, "The relationship managers were encouraged to go out and take care of the client and manage the relationship, not manage the money. I had access to smart outside money managers. These were fantastic people with great pedigrees, working for fantastic firms, and they managed money pretty well. However, when you stacked those managers' returns up against their benchmark indexes, it was really nothing to brag about. What I also realized was that their way of investing was extremely tax-inefficient."

Armstrong gives an example, saying, "If I had a client whose asset-allocation strategy required a large-cap growth equity manager and a large-cap value manager, I would outsource those pieces of the asset allocation to two different asset managers, one to a large-cap growth manager in New York, for example, and one to a large-cap value manager in San Diego, California. They would be the best managers I could find. The problem was that the one hand wasn't shaking the other. The person in the middle was me, the relationship manager. So if the large-cap growth manager was selling XYZ because he didn't think it was a good stock for his strategy anymore, and at the same time, the large-cap value manager was buying XYZ because he thought it was a great value, I had a massive wash-sale problem on my hands. That's because the one manager was not talking to the other, they certainly were not talking to me, and I was not doing the trades." This is an extremely tax-inefficient way to manage money. Additionally there were always a significant amount of short-term trades done, which resulted in short-term gains, which were more taxable events."

Another problem was that for every asset-class exposure his clients needed, such as small-cap growth, small-cap value, or international, he had relationships with many managers and none of them were talking to each other, setting up potential duplications and lack of true diversification. To move money around between accounts, Armstrong would have to have them sell stocks out of one account and buy in another account, and it got to be a real hassle for everyone involved, especially the accountants. Also, to tally up the trades for reporting purposes, including calculating gains and losses, created an additional expense for his clients in addition to the fee charged for portfolio management.

"I looked at it and asked myself, 'How much value are these managers actually adding over time, versus the index?'" Armstrong says. "Albeit unscientific," he says, "through casual observation and reading the research reports of the people who actually did the hard-core research, I came to the conclusion that most of the managers weren't doing a whole lot better than their benchmark index was. So what was I doing? Why was I introducing this extra layer of fees to clients?" Armstrong says clients were getting statements that had 350 pages of holdings, because a small-cap growth manager might hold 120 different stocks and exhibit very high turnover on an annual basis.

Portfolio Management Got Simpler and More Effective with ETFs

Armstrong, back in 2002, asked himself, "What if I took the same client asset allocation and rather than outsource to third-party money managers, I just bought the 12 to 15 different ETFs that track the performance of the benchmark that those managers are trying to beat in the first place? So I just set up this little strategy for myself." Armstrong set up the strategy and tested it to see whether it would work. In his IRA, Armstrong closed his managed portfolios, and bought ETFs according to his asset allocation.

One day, one of Armstrong's biggest clients walked into his office and asked him what he should do with "a bunch of cash I've got laying around?" The client was the CFO of a publicly traded company, very sophisticated in money matters and investing. Armstrong went through a number of strategies, such as "sprinkling it around" across his various existing money managers, investing in some new private equity offerings, and buying some hedge funds. The client kept shaking his head and saying "naah." So Armstrong, without consulting with his partners, displayed a spreadsheet that he had, and showed the client what he had been doing with ETFs in his own account, and asked the client, "What do you think of this—have you ever heard of ETFs?"

Armstrong told his client, "Here's my strategy—basically, I'm just going to be buying 12 to 15 different ETFs. First, my asset allocation says I should have exposure to eight core ETFs—large-cap growth, large-cap value, small-cap growth, small-cap value, mid-cap growth, and mid-cap value, so I'll always have those six. I will decide how much to over- or under-weight each of those six based on the current economic cycle. Plus I'll always have two international. In addition to those eight, I'm going to buy three out of the ten sectors of the S&P 500. I'll also have some exposure to other non-S&P sectors such as commodities, REITs, or something slightly tactical without overdoing it." Armstrong explained to his client that through this strategy he was going to have all the asset classes that all managers were trying to beat.

By adjusting the weightings to the eight main ETFs, adding the three S&P 500 sectors, and selecting a few other ETFs to add some tactical management, he would have a portfolio that was well positioned to do better than the S&P 500 on a total return basis over the next 12 to 18 months, based on where the market was in the business cycle.

"He looks at me," Armstrong says, "here's a corporate executive, a CFO of a publicly traded company who's had his money managed on Wall Street for a long time, and he says, 'This is the best idea I've ever heard anybody on Wall Street talk to me about in the past 20 years. I want to do it.'" The client not only wanted to do it with his spare cash, he wanted all his funds converted into the strategy. After the client left, Armstrong said to his partners, "We're on to something here."

From Outsourcing to In-Sourcing

For the next 12 months Armstrong and his partners moved every client away from outsourcing assets to third-party money managers, a very popular procedure on Wall Street at the time, and put the funds into their new ETF strategy. Armstrong says, "We in-sourced the funds. I said, 'I'm a CFA charterholder, I'm going to be the portfolio manager, I'm going to pick 12 to 15 ETFs based on where we are in the business cycle, and we're going to manage these portfolios ourselves going forward."

The clients now had 12 securities, not almost 400, and could look on one page and see exactly how well each position was performing.

JForlines Global Investment Management

John A. Forlines III (Chairman and CIO) www.jaforlines.com

JForlines Global (JFG) uses a global, top-down macro view in constructing portfolios. It attempts to identify long-range global trends, but tactically adjusts using the credit cycle as an important guide. To cover client objectives, it offers separately managed accounts available at select brokers and dealers and to registered investment advisors. JFG portfolios are also available through ModelxChange for Retirement Plan Assets. AUM $300 million.

How JFG Approaches the Markets

JFG attempts to identify very long-range global developments, calculate how these developments will affect global economies, and invest in the asset classes that will appreciate as the trends unfold. The firm uses ETFs to express its investment views. Clients' portfolios are adjusted to the shorter-term economic, political, and financial cycle influences, while maintaining its investments for longer-term developments.

JFG feels most of the actively managed mutual funds have failed investors in the last several years. The reasons include the trading, marketing, and administrative costs associated with mutual funds, and the lack of tactical strategies available to investors. Investors have to look beyond buy-and-hold to receive decent returns.

First, JFG derives ideas from analyzing proprietary macro research, combined with 45 financial condition variables. From this, it distills its big picture ideas, which allows JFG to rank asset classes, and decide on its long-term and short-term investment themes. From this broad-brush approach, JFG uses its extensive ETF knowledge to express its investment views, which it has developed from analyzing its choices of sectors, regions, countries, and currencies. The ETFs are then bought according to its models, which consider factors including risk-reward opportunities and market conditions.

Global Top-Down Managers

John Forlines, Chairman and Chief Investment Officer of JFG, says he uses ETFs for specific reasons and that they are efficient tools to use for indexing and other forms of asset allocation. There were two camps that originally used ETFs and that continue to this day. In one camp are professionals such as hedge fund and technical analysis managers, and ETFs allow them to easily move in and out of markets. In the second camp are managers like JFG who use fundamental macro and credit cycle analysis in portfolio construction. He says, "Our camp is more traditional in the sense that it is rooted in global allocation principles. That is, three asset classes should be in a portfolio: commodities, fixed income, and equities, and you can obtain that balance very efficiently through ETFs, particularly over the last five years where there has been a lot of development in the product area."

JFG looks at many of the same things that traditional global-allocation managers such as Jeremy Grantham look at when assembling multi-asset portfolios. John Forlines has been influenced by the work of Grantham, who is known for his prediction of market and economic bubbles. One of his major investment concepts is *reversion to the mean*, which is the belief that asset classes and markets move in cycles from historical highs and lows.

JFG believes that when implementing its top-down, global-macro philosophy, exchange-traded products are cheap and efficient tools. A top-down, global-macro approach looks at the big picture, such as global economic trends and financial outlooks, versus bottom-up investing, which uses stock picking, without much consideration to overall economic trends. Forlines says if his firm were given $1 million to invest for a client, and if $1 million were also given to a traditional global-allocation manager, Forlines would have an advantage because the traditional manager would need to have offices in maybe 20 different places throughout the world. They would have to have "boots on the ground," which is to say, research people to go see companies and speak with the CFOs and others with knowledge about companies that are investment candidates.

Forlines would only have to consider his global economic analysis to come up with the geographic regions that he wants exposure in, and look at the JFG credit analysis and other factors to determine in what region he wants to assemble portfolios. Through its methods JFG can put together effective portfolios using 12 to 22 positions, whereas the traditional stock picking, global-allocation portfolio manager needs about 1,000 different positions using stocks and bonds. "Top-down, global-macro analysis is not a new investment management concept," Forlines says. "It has proven to be a way to achieve good returns with less risk over various investment cycles. What is new is that exchange-traded products make this investment style incredibly efficient and cost-effective."

Asset Classes Include Commodities

Commodities are one of the three asset-risk categories that JFG uses in portfolios. Commodities have run up in 2010–2011, and Forlines still believes in this asset class, although is less enthusiastic about its prices than when they were selling at lower levels. "You could make the case," he says, "that there's room in a multi-asset-class portfolio almost always for equities, and there's room most of the time, I'd say the vast majority of the time, for fixed-income exposure. There are times in portfolios when you really have to be wary, and perhaps even not be in commodities."

Forlines doesn't think that this is one of those times, at least not yet, and he is always adjusting his thinking and ready to be out of the asset class when it seems not beneficial to have the exposure. JFG likes agriculture and energy exposure a lot, but is figuring that in the future there will be mean reversion, which can be especially true in the commodity asset class. Commodities in general lend themselves to bubbles, so there are times to have slight exposure or be out of them. JFG is careful when putting portfolios together to not get caught being in commodities at the wrong time.

In its *Advisor Update*, which JFG prepares for its advisors and fiduciary clients, JFG points out that information overload is one of the worst pitfalls for investors and their advisors. So JFG keeps things simple, and presents only two thoughts and two charts in most

Updates. In a recent *Update* it was pointed out that credit cycles are accommodative at some point to different asset classes. But accommodation can lead to an asset class being led into a bubble, and then the mean reversion corrects this bubble. So investors must be careful, and JFG monitors positions in its three asset classes constantly, especially its commodities exposure.

As far as monitoring its exposure, Forlines says, "The way we do our process, we rely heavily on credit analysis, so all three asset classes are subject to heavy dollops of this work. If monetary policy in a certain region, or as it applies to a certain sector, is easy, and if there is a steep yield curve, most likely you will see commodity prices in general do well." Forlines also thinks that, similarly, looking at the same type of impact that credit has, that a case can be made that all types of commodities will not run all at the same time or rate.

He points at the housing market as a case where "blips" in credit policy can have real impact on a sector or asset class. The housing market, in Forlines view, is a credit-driven market that is currently in bad condition because of mistakes made by policy makers, among others. In the present credit cycle, one in which cheap money is offered, Forlines thinks certain commodities, such as agriculture, energy, and some metals should do quite well. Because of credit difficulties, this time real estate will not participate, at least not until later.

In the three asset classes that Forlines uses, commodities are the most relevant in the general heading of alternative investments. Alternatives can also include other asset classes, such as timber and real estate. Forlines is using broad strokes and calling the asset classes commodities, but at any time the asset class used will vary.

How John Forlines Came to Invest the Way He Does

Forlines invests using macro-analysis to guide him to big opportunities. There were two big lessons that Forlines picked up early: investing global and the effects of credit on markets. He says, "I spent most of my early career at J.P. Morgan, a global firm, and I remember at J.P. Morgan that 50 percent of my training class was international. So I had a real good grounding early in that if you're going to look at any type of investing, you need to be global. Also, the early days of J.P. Morgan taught me very important lessons about applying credit analysis to every asset class, and the importance of it in economic cycles."

He spent a lot of time early in his career on the sell side rather than on the buy side, and that convinced him that an investor can achieve most of the needed benefits by being a top-down sector and regional investor, rather than by analyzing companies as a bottom-up stock picker. There were times on the sell side when he found it difficult to know what a company was doing, and if he couldn't understand a company with his training, maybe there was something wrong with bottoms-up stock picking analysis as it is applied to many companies. Bottoms-up analysis, Forlines believes, is now the province of select hedge funds and niche sector and style managers, and it certainly hasn't served the broad mutual fund community over the last 12 years.

These factors led him to embrace multi-asset global portfolio investing and to concentrate on how these portfolios would be affected by credit.

Advice to Investors

"Off the top of my head," Forlines says, "I would advise investors to construct a diversified portfolio of index products, like ETFs, with the three asset classes, which is a great way to go relative to all the other stuff that is out there." Forlines says that the mutual fund industry, which was big back in the 1970s, was built to provide diversity to people. Since then, the industry got caught up in the Wall Street cost structure, so that expenses going into mutual funds became quite high. This high-cost structure and lack of tactical agility in adverse credit cycles has hurt the performances of mutual funds, and lessened investor returns.

Forlines advocates simple multi-asset class diversification through index products, which ETFs provide.

What to Invest in Now

Forlines thinks that after three years of difficulty, the U.S. economy is slowly starting to grind ahead, which is a big development, considering the near-death experience of just a couple years ago. Typically, he points out, when economies as large as that of the U.S. begin an expansion phase, the industrial, energy, and technology sectors are at the forefront and tend to do well. As a global investor, these same sectors may not work as well in other places, because other countries may be in a different part of the credit cycle or business cycle.

ClearRock Capital

Mark Eshman (Co-founder, Chairman, and Chief Investment Officer) www.clearrockcapital.com

The ClearRock portfolio managers believe in their time-tested approach of developing a broadly and globally diversified portfolio to help their clients reach their investment goals. There are five Clear-Rock Model Portfolios, which use ETFs, and are designed to match their clients' market risk tolerance. AUM $300 million.

ClearRock Puts Its Clients First

ClearRock constructs portfolios to solve the question of what will work best for its clients. It pursues creating life-long relationships with clients, works at providing superior client experiences, and has built its systems and processes from the perspective of its customers' needs and sensibilities. ClearRock believes that its clients rely on them to be advocates in the investment marketplace. Many of its clients view the company as being their Chief Investment Officer, and its clients ask for ClearRock's advice on a variety of investment concerns.

ClearRock believes that this fiduciary model, where responsibility and accountability support a dedication to the interests of its clients, is superior to alternative models. Its strategic thinking is based on the conviction that a tactical, indexed approach is superior to and more effective than an actively managed approach. Everything it does in its portfolio management activity is structured around broadly diversified and proprietary asset-allocation modeling of ETFs.

ClearRock Has its Own Investment Process

ClearRock does not rely on research coming from Wall Street but conducts its own top-down proprietary research process. Its process is rooted in market trends as well as macro-economic data such as inflation, interest rates, and global trade. ClearRock determines how these trends will affect each asset class. ClearRock believes that the principal way to add value is through its asset-allocation selection. The model portfolios are designed with the goal of preserving and growing capital through delivering equity-like returns with lower-than-market volatility over the long term.

Portfolio decisions are first determined through the results gathered from ClearRock's data collection and analysis process. ClearRock does its own market analysis, and all market data and analyses are passed through each step of its research process. In its portfolio modeling, it conducts data evaluation for relevance and priority, and makes its asset class and sector investment selections. It also conducts risk control and portfolio optimization and scenario analysis, which leads it to factors such as efficient portfolio construction and portfolio stress testing. The managers screen a universe of more than 1,100 ETFs for tax efficiency, expenses, liquidity, and tracking errors, and then they select ETFs that provide the desired asset class, sector, and country exposure. They continuously conduct model analysis and evaluation, including a weekly investment committee meeting and periodic portfolio rebalancing.

Asset Allocation Using ETFs

Mark Eshman, who co-founded ClearRock Capital and is chairman and CIO of the firm, says that the traditional brokerage model is broken. "Wall Street is the last industry in the country that is selling an overpriced product that does not work," he says. Eight years after Eshman opened a branch for a major wire-house in Sun Valley, Idaho, the firm decided to close the branch. He had opportunities to open a branch for other firms, but Eshman thought moving his clients into another Wall Street firm was not in his clients' best interest. "My clients deserved better," Eshman remembers saying as he decided against moving to another brokerage firm. He decided he could do a better job if he created his own firm and operated it in a purely client-focused way.

He has been in the money-management business for more than 31 years and has spent a great deal of that time working with nonprofit organizations. "The one thing I learned in the nonprofit world," he says, "is that large endowments and foundations manage their money much better, on balance, than individual investors." After reading several books and researching different investment strategies, Eshman says that "the light bulb blinked on and the stars lined up, and I envisioned how I was going to reinvent myself without going to another big firm. I decided to set up a registered investment advisory firm and embrace the tenets I had learned."

Eshman explains, "It's all about asset allocation, not about expensive mutual funds, and it's not about hiring active managers who empirically have a really lousy track record of even meeting their benchmarks, which they are paid very well to beat. It's really about creating the appropriate risk-adjusted diversified model using index funds." After considering different investment securities including closed-end and open-end funds as well as ETFs, Eshman and his partners arrived at the concept that they would have five risk models suitable for different types of clients' objectives. They wanted to strip away the complexities of investing, which they thought did not do their clients much good.

"We decided to approach investing very clearly with our clients about how their money is being invested, how we will report to them, and give them a very robust service experience. What they wanted was something that was uncomplicated and clear. They wanted a simple and straightforward investment process, they wanted our interests aligned with theirs, and they simply did not want to lose money," Eshman says.

He says that unlike what investors expected of their brokers in the past—hot tips, the trade of the day, flipping stocks by the hour, hot new IPOs—investors really want their money to grow slowly over time, with low volatility, fair fees, and tax efficiency. ClearRock has a disciplined investment process, which starts with an assessment of the client's needs. From these needs, ClearRock and the client determine which portfolio makes the most sense, choosing from Conservative, Moderate, Aggressive, Global Growth, or Global Income.

ClearRock uses a client-centric approach, and says it is an uncomplicated process that is rooted in the old style of giving a client a broadly diversified portfolio. Diversification matters because the client's portfolio does not depend on any one scenario working out. It believes that investors have a hard time making good asset-allocation decisions and note that just before the dot-com crash in 1999, investors pulled their money out of bonds and put it into stocks. In 2009, 12 months before the market had a huge rally, investors pulled their money out of stocks and put it into bonds.

ClearRock works to achieve this broad diversification through a research-intensive, multi-asset class portfolio using all ETFs. Its process starts with a deep dive into its clients' financial needs and financial objectives, which are documented in a personal investment policy statement. It then determines, with the client, which portfolio best meets the client's goals, as articulated in the personal investment policy statement. It monitors the portfolios weekly in its weekly investment policy meetings and communicates with its clients regularly to make sure they understand how the portfolio is performing in comparison to their financial goals.

ClearRock has a weekly investment committee meeting in which it identifies the macro-economic factors that affect its portfolios. ClearRock reviews portfolios with its clients quarterly, and rebalances portfolios semi-annually. Eshman says the ClearRock approach can be described as "tactically managed indexing." He thinks that ETFs are the best securities for many reasons, including real-time pricing, transparency, liquidity, and says that "the tax efficiencies of ETFs are pretty spectacular, too, especially when compared to using active managers."

Research Is ClearRock's Secret Sauce

Eshman says, "A third of our clients are small endowments and foundations with under $50 million in assets. Another third of our clients are retirement plans where we are advising their plan participants and plan sponsors on asset allocation. We are already doing the work on asset allocation, so we can leverage that for 401(k) plans. We're now at the point where we can offer our Model Portfolios on 401(k) platforms. People can select the ClearRock Model Portfolios as an investment option for their plans. The last third of our clients are individual investors who we serve directly and through other advisors. We are in the midst of rolling out on new platforms where wealth managers and other financial advisors can access our Model Portfolios on their firms' separately managed account platforms."

Eshman thinks that most individual investors are not well-equipped to construct ETF portfolios. When ClearRock was started, it was proprietary about its strategies and didn't want to share its

Model Portfolios with others. Eshman says he doesn't have that fear now, pointing out that "the secret sauce is not the Model. The secret sauce is the research behind the Model. There is nothing new under the sun, and there are things that differentiate us from other managers who construct model portfolios. What we do is top-down, macroeconomic research, and we use real-world data in our straightforward transparent process. Because we make periodic tactical shifts in our allocations due to economic data, our Model today might look quite different from our Model two months from now."

ClearRock's Model construction begins with an analysis of the data collected in its ClearRock Macroeconomic Dashboard. It tracks more than 20 macro-economic data points on a weekly basis and relates these points to the different asset classes in which the company invests. The asset classes it currently uses are fixed income, domestic equities, foreign equities, emerging markets, real estate, and commodities.

From its economic data, it determines how much it weights each asset class. For example, it evaluates the retail sales number and determines its impact on foreign equities or domestic equities. It also assigns a number to the other data points, such as new home sales, unemployment claims, and oil prices, to determine sector or country weightings within each asset class. For example, if the data implies expectations for higher inflation, it will increase its allocation to commodity-rich countries such as Australia and Canada. For fixed income, it would over-weight TIPs and under-weight noninflation-protected bonds. Its process leads to what it believes to be efficient portfolio construction. It performs scenario analysis and stress tests its Models before doing its final optimization.

Eshman says most individual investors aren't inclined to do this type of research on their own and probably will not achieve the same outcomes as ClearRock. He says, "The world changes every day. Inputs change every day. On a week-to-week basis, maybe we don't make a lot of changes in the portfolio, but certainly month-to-month we do. Every couple of months, we tweak the portfolio because new data might cause us to reduce exposure in something, for example, from 5 percent to 2 percent. Most investors, even if they're retired, don't want to do that much work even if they could. They'd rather pay someone a modest fee to manage their money in that fashion."

Even if an investor is a buy-and-hold type, he doesn't want to buy and hold and lose money, Eshman says. He says buy-and-hold is essentially dead. "With a tactically managed low-turnover portfolio, you can really increase your rate of return. By simply being more tactical—not as a day trader or trying to time the market—you can perform better than simply holding stocks," he says. He notes that ClearRock has a low turnover rate at about 32 percent a year. "Today's tremendous volatility renders buy-and-hold virtually useless in serious portfolio management."

Accuvest Global Advisors

David Garff, CIMA (President) www.accuvest.com

Accuvest has developed expertise managing portfolios with its proprietary core-satellite-tactical methodology. It also uses its proprietary factor-based country ranking model to manage top-down global equity portfolios. AUM $350 million.

Accuvest's Emphasis on Country ETFs

Accuvest does a variety of different things as it manages accounts using ETFs. Its president, David Garff, says that country ETF picking is the thing that its management has become known for over the last five years. He is the CEO and heads the Investment Committee and Portfolio Management Team. In that capacity, he oversees Accuvest's asset-allocation process, its core, satellite, and tactical portfolio management strategy (CST). CST combines a multi-dimensional view to how each asset affects a portfolio. He also oversees the country selection model, and Accuvest's hedge-fund-of-funds portfolio.

His associate, Brad Jensen, is a senior portfolio manager. Jensen is responsible for investment strategy, asset allocation, and portfolio management.

Garff thinks it's important to have global exposure in portfolios. In his white paper "Global Equity Investing: Do Countries Still Matter?," which is available on the Accuvest website, he makes the point that the majority of investors have a strong home country bias. This is short-sighted, he explains, because both developed countries and emerging market exposure can have a positive effect on portfolio performance.

In his white paper, Garff explores why investors are reluctant to invest overseas. He notes that as defined by the MSCI AC World Index, the U.S. represents only 43 percent of the world market capitalization. This suggests that there is much opportunity outside of the U.S., and investors are leaving much on the table by not participating.

Among the reasons investors have for not investing overseas are such things as political risks and low levels of government regulation. He says that the U.S. has similar shortcomings, such as elections whose outcomes are not known for months and the history of companies hiding poor results through accounting irregularities.

Garff's research has come to the clear conclusion that there are wide differences between among country performances. As a result, diversification and the lowering of portfolio volatility can be gained by multi-country exposure. An investor is probably not giving up performance by reducing his U.S. exposure: The U.S. has not ranked as the top-performing country compared to developed markets one time in the last 20 years.

It is of utmost importance which countries are in an investor's portfolio. Garff found that no country has been dominant in the top-ranking position over the last 20 years. On the other hand, some of the undeveloped countries have done well. Over the past ten years, Indonesia and Peru have been in the top-ten performing markets almost every year, along with seven times for Indonesia and eight times for Peru. Also, the U.K. has not been in the top-ten performing countries in the last 20 years.

Garff started in the investment business when he joined Merrill Lynch in 1992, focusing on retirement plans. His uncle was also with Merrill, and after three years his uncle left to join Smith Barney. Soon after this, Garff left Merrill to join his uncle at Smith Barney, working with high-net worth and institutional clients. In addition to working full time, he attended the Hass School of Business at the University of California, Berkeley. One of Garff's clients was a money manager who was in the process of changing his investment strategy. For ten years the client had managed fixed income portfolios, and because of client demand was beginning to manage equity portfolios.

Garff, when he wasn't attending classes on nights and weekends and studying, helped his client build a multi-manager fund that was constructed as a global equity portfolio that could be used by investors. "We interviewed hundreds of managers," Garff says, "to build an equity portfolio."

Evolution of Country ETF Modeling

For about eight years, Garff worked with his uncle and selected managers, did all sorts of asset-allocation work, including tactical over-weights, regions, sectors, and styles, but the overriding investment style that Garff kept returning to was geographical investing using top-down factors.

At about this time, in the late 1990s, single-country ETFs had come out and people were starting to trade them, but not very heavily. Garff says, "EWU had about $20 million in it for about five years." EWU is the symbol for iShares MSCI United Kingdom ETF, and that amount is very little. "And, interestingly, in 2004, the volume in those securities spiked, and you could actually implement a broad global mandate using single-country ETFs. I had talked for years about wouldn't it be wonderful to just pick the country and get out of the stock picking business? Now I had the opportunity to do it." So, David started Accuvest Global Advisors in 2005.

Accuvest had three things it wanted to accomplish. The first was to build multi-asset class, top-down investing. This is comprised of typical asset-class allocations using stocks, bonds, cash, and alternatives such as commodities and real estate, and building global asset-class allocation portfolios. Garff says that people call this type of investing endowment style, family office portfolios, and other terms. Many terms are used, but the portfolios developed are basically top-down, global exposure.

"The second thing," Garff says, "was for us to build global-equity portfolios using a model that would pick countries, and use single-country ETFs as its implementation. So, no stock picking." The third thing Accuvest wanted to accomplish was a side venture, which is something it still does, acting as an advisor or a new hedge fund-of-fund. In this capacity, it does things such as due diligence and portfolio construction.

Garff and the team at Accuvest Global Advisors talked about the type of model that would best benefit their clients, and it became clear that some things were important. They determined that the model had to be global. They also decided that the portfolio content would be the same for clients no matter where the clients lived. In other words, the countries in the model had to be attractive as investments, no matter if the clients lived in Russia or in Mexico. Accuvest also decided that its strategy had to be something that was disciplined, consistent, and repeatable, and to have these characteristics the strategy would have to be somewhat quantitative in nature.

Garff says, "One of the things we've seen over the years is that managers get a great track record based on doing some good analysis, but also being kind of smarter than the market. And it is really hard to be smarter than the market every single day. Really hard."

Building Long-Term Portfolios That Will Work

Garff and his team at Accuvest Global Advisors, reflecting their proclivities and experience, wanted to stack the market odds in their favor. They do have experience. Garff and Accuvest's Senior Portfolio Manager Brad Jensen pondered how they could build a portfolio of countries where they could minimize style cyclicality. They did not want to be in cycles where they would be right for a while with the risk that they would be wrong for periods of time, and they did not want to be wrong for extended periods of time. Garff had the experience of hiring value managers to handle portfolios back in 1996; value didn't perform and the managers went through a long term of underperformance, all the way into the first quarter of 2000. Some investment committees that Garff had worked for complained that the value managers that Garff had hired had underperformed for three years. The committees didn't want to wait any longer for performance, so Garff had to fire those underperforming managers, simply because their style was the wrong one for the times.

Garff didn't want this risk of being devoted to a certain style, and not being in the right style at the right time and underperforming. Garff and his team also knew that there were styles that worked, and usually worked at any time if used right. For instance, high-momentum investing could be employed and if used correctly, a manager could make it work in almost any market. Fundamental investing could be made to work in most markets. Deep value, growth-at-a-reasonable-price (GARP), and many other strategies could work with the right manager and in many types of markets.

With this in mind, Garff's team began considering the investment strategies they'd seen work over the years and the theoretical and academic ways of viewing alpha, and also how alpha could be extracted from the market. Alpha is a way of expressing the enhanced performance of an investment in relation to its risk. In addition to achieving exposure to alpha-creating factors, the team wanted these factors to deliver diversification aspects into the portfolios. With these goals established, Accuvest started building its portfolios.

Fans of ETFs from the Start

"Ever since the beginning," Garff says, "we've been big fans of ETFs. We have thought about the world from a top-down perspective, and we continue to do this. We are looking for a consistent, disciplined, repeatable way to pick countries so that we can generate outperformance for our clients." Countries, not stocks or sectors, drive everything it does to achieve this end. Accuvest knows, from a research perspective, that country-specific investments are what can cause its portfolios to gain alpha.

Garff points out that there are roughly 194 sovereign nations in the world and there are 77 stock markets. In his experience, almost nobody can name all the markets off the top of their heads, and sometimes people can name 5, 10, or even 15, but after that, they give up trying. You have to have a view on the country to make an investment decision regarding it, and in his opinion, country effects dominate sector effects over time. This is especially true in emerging markets. So, outperformance hinges on being in the right country in the right time.

There is a wide divergence in performance from country to country, Garff says, which is covered in his white paper on the subject. He says that sectors do matter, that global sector investing can be profitable, but of more importance than which sector an investor buys is what country an investor buys. Among other factors, what Accuvest wants to own in its portfolios are countries that show positive relative performance or positive traits.

It takes a lot of work to determine which country ETFs to buy and which to avoid. When David Garff started following country ETFs, there were just a few; now there are several, and not just country ETFs and equity ETFs.

For investors who want international exposure in their portfolios, they have a broad range of options to choose from. There are currency ETFs, international bond ETFs, REIT ETFs, broad overseas ETFs, frontier country ETFs, small-, mid-, and large-cap country and region ETFs, and inverse international ETFs—enhanced by two and three times international ETFs—and the list goes on. In addition to country international ETFs, there are also regional international ETFs.

Accuvest Global Advisors uses only single-country ETF. Its country-modeling research is focused on finding the right countries to be in at the right time, and to be out of the wrong countries when it is best to be out of them.

The Chudom Hayes Wealth Management Group at Morgan Stanley Smith Barney

Kyle Chudom and Eric Hayes (Co-founders and Portfolio Managers) www.morganstanley.com/fa/chudomhayeswealth management

Chudom and Hayes build broad, diversified portfolios using both tactical and strategic asset allocation. To get true diversification, they typically pick sectors for certain time periods and change sectors as markets change. AUM $488 million.

Constructing Portfolios So That Fear Will Not Distort the Investment Process

Kyle Chudom and Eric Hayes, founders and portfolio managers for Chudom Hayes Wealth Management Group, are investment advisor representatives with Morgan Stanley Smith Barney. They offer planning and investment advice and are sensitive to their clients' risk concerns. They set up investment advisory accounts and mange them on a discretionary basis for a fee, which is based on the amount of the assets managed. Their model portfolios almost exclusively use ETFs. They feel that their job is to manage the financial assets of families so that their clients can focus on doing the things that bring joy, meaning, and purpose to their lives. They are sensitive to their clients' hopes and dreams and also know that their clients have a certain amount of fear dealing with financial matters.

They have to deal with clients' fears, because they say fear can drive a well-constructed plan off of its intended target, and ruin results. Everyday headlines provoke fear, and a significant part of their job is to not let fear distract their clients from sticking to their plan. They work with clients to help them develop a plan for long-term investing. Their portfolios are diversified across a broad range of investments. They adjust client exposure based on the risk and return profile of the client and match this to the volatility risk of chosen asset classes. Chudom and Hayes construct portfolios to be defensive in bear markets and to minimize costs and taxes.

Portfolio Construction Uses ETFs

Chudom and Hayes use ETFs for many reasons, including that ETFs are ideal for capturing asset classes, and this helps when constructing asset-allocation strategies. They consider asset allocation a key factor in constructing portfolios to perform and to defend against loss in bear markets. They believe they can add value by compiling the right asset allocation than by actively managing portfolios using individual stocks and bonds. ETFs enable them to lower expenses, they are tax-efficient, and aid in seeking better after-tax returns.

In managing portfolios they use both strategic and tactical approaches, and manage the asset mix by varying the exposure level as the risk and return profiles of asset classes change. They don't believe in a buy-and-hold strategy, and prefer to use their asset-allocation strategy in their attempt to generate superior returns over the long term. Risk is rewarded better in some market periods than in other periods, they say, so they don't have a fixed investment weighting policy. They say that asset classes become overvalued and undervalued over time, so they stay flexible in their choices and change asset classes as conditions warrant. Among their tactical asset-allocation decisions, they analyze the fundamental, technical, and psychological factors affecting the markets.

Chudom and Hayes believe that the stock market, to a certain extent, is a reflection of mass psychology, and they analyze investor sentiment as a means to understanding and anticipating future market moves. Their sentiment analysis measures the degree of investors' bullishness or bearishness, and is valuable at critical market turning points. They use their sentiment analysis as a tool to be contrarians, believing that to be on the opposite side of the crowds is prudent, and that the crowd is on the wrong side of the market at extreme market points.

ETFs Are Central to Chudom Hayes Portfolio Construction

Chudom and Hayes started investing for clients more than 26 years ago and used individual stocks, mutual funds, and money managers. They found that picking individual stocks might not be the best way to manage money, and using mutual funds and money managers, including large-cap, small-cap, and international managers, didn't satisfy their performance desires, either. They came to the conclusion that typically they had one or two managers underperform a benchmark, one or two outperform a benchmark, and the other managers about matched a benchmark performance. The same was true with mutual funds. Consequently, they ended up performing about as well as their benchmarks, and this is not what Hayes and Chudom wanted. Chudom says, "We were paying higher fees, and having greater taxable events for our clients. With ETFs, we were able to lower costs, have liquidity, and diversify across a broad range of asset classes. We knew exactly what we were buying, and potentially we had more tax efficiency."

They believe that portfolio construction is, as Hayes says, "A little bit of science, and a little bit of art. Our philosophy centered around a number of points. We thought investors should consider having exposure to a diverse group of asset classes at all times, and we thought portfolio risk could be reduced by combining various asset classes. So, we take a very active approach in managing the asset mix for our clients by varying the level of exposure as the risk and return profiles for the individual asset classes or investments change. We just simply feel that a policy of fixed investment weighting fails to account for the fact that risk is much better rewarded in some investment climates and not better rewarded in other climates."

Different Portfolios for Different Risk Profiles

Chudom and Hayes have three basic models for investing, and the models are constructed using ETFs. They say that the number of models will probably increase, and their present models range from very conservative all the way up to a model that owns primarily equities. "In all of our models," Hayes says, "we have fixed income exposure, implemented all with ETFs. We have U.S. equity exposure, and the asset classes include domestic large-cap, small-cap, and mid-cap exposure. The international equity component includes global large-, small-, and mid-cap exposure." The portfolios also have emerging markets exposure, and one of the portfolios holds alternative investments. The company presently holds REIT ETFs, and in the past, it held precious metals, and is constantly considering other alternatives.

When Chudom and Hayes sit down with clients, they seek to uncover what the client is attempting to accomplish from a planning aspect and an investment aspect. From there Chudom and Hayes match up not only the client's goal set, but also the client's risk tolerance. About risk tolerance, Hayes says, "Typically we'll try to characterize that conversation around how, on a scale of one to ten, with ten being the most aggressive or the most volatile portfolio, we'll ask, Mr. or Mrs. Client, where do you think you are? We'll start to build a discussion around that. And then ultimately, as that discussion evolves, along with the client, we'll figure out which portfolio they will fit well in, not only to achieve their long-term investment objectives, but also how they feel about volatility."

Hayes says in the terrible market storm of 2008 to 2009, discussing fear and volatility with clients on an ongoing basis helped get their clients through that time. He says that investors with experience of only bull markets certainly have a much different perspective about the risk they can handle compared with someone who has a tremendous amount of experience and has gone through a few market cycles. The experienced investor understands volatility both on the upside and the downside. Chudom and Hayes speak with clients about every six months to review portfolio performance and progress and to explain what they are doing in the portfolio models and why. They also address the current risk and volatility.

"One of our big beliefs is that we're not just here to help them grow their money over the long run, but we're here to defend their capital, to defend their money when things gets rough, and part of that is structuring correct behavior." Hayes says, "We can have wonderful investment models, but if we can't construct and balance investors' behavior, it probably doesn't mean a whole lot in the long run because they will make the wrong decision at absolutely the wrong time."

The portfolios constructed by Chudom and Hayes "will consistently change based on market conditions," Chudom says. Currently the most conservative model has 62 percent of its assets in fixed income and 38 percent in equity ETFs. "But that portfolio," Chudom says, "at one point had as much as 75 percent in fixed income and as little as 51 percent back in 2007. We typically own between 12 and 20 ETFs in each of the models, and that is in contrast to our aggressive model, which has 9 percent in fixed income and 91 percent in equities. But that aggressive model, at one point, had 45 percent in fixed income." The company also has alternative investments in its portfolios, depending on market conditions and the relative value in the asset classes.

Managing Instincts That Are Dominated by Feelings of Fear

First and foremost, Chudom and Hayes clearly define a client's goals and objectives. They feel that the client entrusts money to them and they want to know what the client is trying to accomplish with this money. They stay in constant touch with clients to make sure goals and risk tolerance haven't changed. "What affects returns more than anything," Chudom says, "is, in fact, fear. We have to control our clients' fear because if it is not controlled, it can be the main cause of failure in many financial plans. Psychology and investor behavior have made the biggest impact on return that our clients will see. And those who continue to follow our advice, we believe, in the long run will be better off because we're trying to manage the behavior of our clients because instinctively people sometimes want to get out, when, in fact, there are great opportunities to get into the market."

Managing their clients' behavior becomes especially important in market pullbacks. In the down market in 2008–2009, Chudom says, "That is when we provided the value to our clients. We got many phone calls from clients asking if they should remain in the market, and wouldn't we be better if we moved all of our money to cash?" Chudom and Hayes reminded clients what their goals and objectives were, the plan that they had constructed to meet those goals, and made sure that those goals hadn't changed. Chudom says their main function is to coach clients to not pay attention to the headlines or the conflicting commentary they hear on the news channels, and instead stick to their goals.

Chudom and Hayes say that in constructing portfolios, they employ a blend of factors, encompassing a strategic allocation and a tactical asset allocation. One of the strategic factors is that the models always have some cash in equities, and this is because of the belief that it is impossible to time the market perfectly. They believe that there are periods when equities are on sale and offer good value, and at those times, they will over-weight equities. When they believe equities are priced too high, they reduce their portfolios' equity weighting.

One Capital Management, LLC

Patrick J. Bowen (President) www.onecapital.com

One Capital has a clear mission, which is to help clients achieve their objectives at the least possible risk. Included in this is the mandate to protect client assets and provide peace of mind while building globally balanced portfolios. AUM $490 million.

Using ETFs for Client Portfolios

Patrick Bowen, president of One Capital Management, says, "We're a wealth management firm with a proprietary investment solution, so we're not outsourcing to other managers for any of the investment management part of what we do. The lone exception to that is our use of ETFs. We do not manufacture ETFs here; we treat them as another security, a security that represents some sectors, industries, asset classes, and some stripe, if you will, of an asset class."

One Capital constructs its multi-asset class portfolios by blending active management of global large-cap equities with the use of ETFs and fixed income. ETFs are used to access capital markets and asset classes to reduce risk and increase portfolio returns. The company believes that global deployment enhances the probability of achieving its clients' wealth management objectives, which is to strive for each client's target rate of return by accessing and adding high real-return assets.

One Capital Management does not use ETFs that offer leverage or other more esoteric offerings, but "straight vanilla" ETFs. From its first use of ETFs, it has been for building a globally structured multi-asset class portfolio from U.S. large-cap down to micro-cap, going outside of the U.S. to developed markets, large-cap down to small-cap, then to emerging markets, including small-cap. On the fixed-income side, it generally uses ETFs for smaller accounts only, but it will also use ETFs for higher-return fixed income, such as high-yield bonds. One Capital also uses ETFs for real estate investments such as REITs, both inside and outside of the U.S. It wants to utilize low-correlation asset classes and regularly rebalance. Bowen feels that the term "portfolio completion" might fit somewhat in describing how the company uses ETFs. It uses ETFs in asset classes where it might make cost efficiencies in inefficient markets. There are active managers in the small-cap space, micro-cap space, and other spaces that declare they have a high likelihood of adding value because they operate in an inefficient market. Bowen's view is that maybe the active managers will add value and maybe the active managers won't add value, but there is a cost to the way they try to add value. It is true that some markets, such as micro-cap, may be inefficient, and spreads in small-cap, micro-cap, and overseas securities tend to be wider then they are in the large-cap spaces. But "the cost to invest, just by setting up brokerage accounts in foreign countries, is expensive, along with the trading costs that are directly related to each transaction."

"All of those things become inefficiencies, and make it more expensive to get access to micro-cap or small-cap overseas or emerging markets, or other like investments. So, our belief is that we would rather be as efficient as we possibly can everywhere we turn in the portfolio," Bowen says. "We use ETFs to fill those buckets for the asset allocation in the structure of the portfolio. We don't use them in the large-cap space because we have far greater opportunity to tax trade. We are in the private client portfolio management space, for high-net worth clients, so we have to, as best we can, maximize the tax efficiency of the portfolio."

Bowen says that ETFs are tax-efficient, but with individual stocks, you have more opportunity to realize losses, whereas with ETFs, you must sell the whole sector or asset class. Even when a sector is up and you are holding ETFs, there might be individual stocks in that sector that are down, but with ETFs, you cannot sell these stocks to harvest losses.

One Capital Management is a stock-picking manager that uses ETFs to augment portfolios. Mostly it picks large-cap stocks and dips down to mid-caps, or it stays on the border between large-cap and mid-cap. About 60 percent of its managed portfolios is for U.S. clients and the other 40 percent is for Canadian citizens. So, One Capital has single stock names in the Canadian large-cap and mid-cap space and it has single stocks in the U.S. large-cap space, dipping into the U.S. mid-cap space. Canadian and U.S. large-caps are different. U.S. large-caps are much larger and there are many more U.S. names in that space than Canadian names.

One Capital has been managing money for many financial advisors over the years, and these advisors said that they like what One Capital does, they like the structured portfolios, and they have smaller accounts, so what can One Capital do for smaller accounts? To fill this niche One Capital created five ETF-only portfolios, which they offer through advisors for smaller accounts. These portfolios follow One Capital's philosophy and are built following their structure.

Stock-Picking Strategies

One Capital takes a top-down macro view of the world and makes decisions about where it wants to allocate funds across the globe and what sectors it wants to over-weight and under-weight. It can make these considerations based on its CIO's economic view and forecast. The next step is its evaluation process, in which it can select the stocks that it wants put into its portfolios. There are two pieces to the securities-selection process, which is done by its research team. The research team first selects securities based on value, deep value, and growth at a reasonable price. From these names, it goes into the second piece of its process, which is blending these securities together to make a growth and value portfolio. It blends these names from different criteria because it feels that over time, growth and value behave differently in the short term, thereby providing diversification down to the style level. This strategy also pertains to its ETF approach. When both growth and value are available in an asset class, it uses both styles and blends these ETFs together.

One Capital starts its portfolio-building process from the top down, deciding what asset class it wants to have exposure to and how much it wants to allocate to each class. Then it looks at countries and individual sectors to make its stock selections. From the top down, it looks at how these asset classes have behaved relative to one another historically, and the volatility of each asset class by itself and relative to one another. It looks at the most efficient allocation it can build among those asset classes, which decides how much exposure to have in large-cap, how much in mid-cap, and how much in small-cap. It also decides how much exposure it wants to the U.S. market, how much to the developed overseas markets, and how much in emerging markets.

For example, say that One Capital for its U.S. equity exposure wants 60 percent large-cap, 15 percent mid-cap, and 25 percent between small- and micro-cap. Also assume it finds that large-cap has outperformed small-cap over the last five years. It will then determine the relative valuation of large-cap to small-cap and decide whether it is getting value. If large-cap outperformed small-cap over the last five years, it has to decide whether there is a significant, compelling reason that large-cap can continue to outperform. It would also determine if it is more likely that the underperforming asset class, which in this example is small-cap, will outperform in the ensuing period, sort of a reversion to the mean.

Valuation Models to Calculate Desired Exposure

At that point in the process, One Capital refers to its valuation models to determine what the better exposure is, small-cap or large-cap. Unless earnings growth for large-cap have dramatically outstripped earnings growth for small-cap, there is no valid reason to continue an expanded exposure for large-cap. The assumption is that momentum has caused large-cap to outperform, and that it's reasonable to assume that small-cap will have its day and that more exposure to small-cap is prudent. Bowen says at that point, they will go back and determine where they are, at least on the margins. His decision making would run something like this: "Well, we were 25 percent small- and micro-, where should we be now? Let's trim a little bit, maybe about five percent, maybe ten off of the large-cap space and move that into small- and micro-, and make a little bit more of a weighted bet on the asset class." This is how small- and micro- would be increased. This process is duplicated no matter what asset class is considered, such as U.S. versus overseas markets, versus emerging markets, or versus another.

An example of how One Capital determines asset-class exposure is its changing weighting of real estate. For about ten years, One Capital used REITs for this exposure, and started out with about a 10 percent allocation. About six years ago, it went down to a 5 percent allocation because REITs massively outperformed, whereas their valuations didn't make sense to the firm. After about a year and a half, the company trimmed its holdings to 2.5 percent, which is where they are today. Over the last year or so, the company has debated moving the allocation back to 5 percent. Bowen wishes it would've increased exposure back in the beginning of 2010, because REITs have been one of the best performing asset classes since that period. But back in early 2010, he explains, "There was not enough compelling reason to think that real estate was going to outperform, other than just saying that it was so beat up that at some point, it will come back."

One Capital Management uses valuation methods to determine sector exposure. It takes its global macro overlay and decides which industries it thinks will benefit from the current economic environment and also which industries will benefit one, two, and three years out. From its valuations, it makes its over-weights and under-weights.

As an example, Bowen says that in 2008, financials were badly battered, and that One Capital had some exposure in the sector: "Heading into the fall of 2008, we were already in. In November of '08, we increased our exposure to a pretty significant over-weight in financials because of the inherent values, and valuations relative to our forecasted expectations of earnings growth over the next one, two, and three years." One Capital believed financials looked "incredibly cheap," and it over-weighted the sector. When it bought in November 2008, One Capital had to suffer for four months, "pretty painful suffering," he says, before that sector turned. The tail end of the financial sector downward spiral was fierce, and then the sector snapped back beginning in March 2009. Bowen says, "Our clients were handsomely rewarded for their patience."

Investment Advice

Bowen is reluctant to make an overall stock or sector call, because if someone is investing on his own, and he follows Bowen's advice to buy something, when does the investor get out? So, Bowen won't make that call, but he does advise investors to build portfolios and be sure to rebalance back to asset-allocation targets periodically. The investor has to go through some exercise to figure out his risk tolerance and return needs.

He thinks an equity portfolio should be broadly diversified between U.S. stocks, large-, small-, mid-, and micro-. Also the portfolio should have overseas stocks, including large-cap and small-cap. There should be exposure in the emerging markets space. In the fixed-income portion, there should be high-yield bonds in the portfolio.

High-yield bonds at times tend to perform similarly to equities and additionally pay a high interest rate, which helps overall portfolio return. Also, investors should have an allocation to emerging markets because that is where the real economic growth will be over the next 10 to 20 years. "We're not going to see economic growth like that in developed markets," he says.

Cabot Money Management, Inc.

Robert T. Lutts, President, Chief Investment Officer
www.ecabot.com

Cabot understands that each of its clients has different financial needs, depending on factors including their stage of life. Cabot's team of advisors tailors its clients' investments to match their needs to their risk profiles. AUM $500 million.

Cabot Considers Risk When Setting Up Client Portfolios

Cabot Money Management's investment-management process is grounded in the belief that long-term investing shouldn't be based on tips or hunches, but on strategies in which research and analysis are used to quantify fundamentals. It combines this with asset-class, risk-reward factors. Cabot uses a disciplined approach to investing, resisting the impulse to get carried away by the euphoria of a market at its peak. It is not crippled by fear at market bottoms. Cabot's team is comprised of tactical investment advisors who attempt to reduce its clients' market exposure during extended weak market times. At those times, it trims positions, raises portfolio cash levels, and uses its loss guidelines to help protect principal and lower risk levels.

Cabot Money Management believes that the key to long-term investment success lies in managing portfolio risk through the consistent and disciplined application of its developed investment philosophy. The client's interest and goals come first, and Cabot's financial counselors work with clients to determine and apply an appropriate asset-allocation and investment strategy to match the client's needs and risk profiles. When setting up a portfolio, Cabot reviews the client's overall financial strategy and considers events that can negatively affect the portfolio, attempting to minimize obstacles to the portfolio's goal.

There are several kinds of investment risk, including stock risk and market risk. These risks can often be reduced by diversification, but diversification doesn't merely mean owning a number of different stocks. True diversification is obtained through owning multiple asset classes of domestic and international equities, fixed-income investments, cash, and alternative classes. Cabot uses gold, commodities, and natural resource securities for its alternative investments.

Cabot Has Diversified and Grown

Robert T. Lutts, president and CIO, says that Cabot was founded as a wealth-management firm about 28 years ago and was an outgrowth of his father's business, which was the Cabot Market Letter. The Market Letter got its start identifying value in high-growth U.S. stocks and has branched out to advising clients in China and many other places. Lutts learned from his father the basic principles of investing. Lutts says that at first Cabot Money Management managed only aggressive stock portfolios, and Cabot grew and shrunk as the markets grew and shrunk. Five years after Cabot Money Management was founded, the company started offering mutual fund accounts and managed those accounts with several different strategies. It offered a high-growth equity, a conservative equity, and a bond strategy. Cabot started a bond market program that offered a high-yield bond strategy, which turned out to be very successful. Cabot continued growing with its bond fund and other strategies.

When the ETF market developed, it started using them by running ETF models to identify ones with the best momentum. "My dad used momentum to identify growth stocks, and he would stay in them during the very highest growth phase. I'm like that, too," Lutts says. Cabot is diversified now, and it can't manage all of its assets in the high-growth space. "It's too much octane and a little too volatile for folks," Lutts says, "so we have more conservative money as well. Now we have a full wealth-management offering. We do taxes for clients, we do estate planning, we do insurance work, and financial planning for our clients to have their money work for them over an intended period of time."

Cabot's business has evolved and Lutts says that it is true to its basic principles, is open-minded to change, and is looking for new avenues to grow and new asset classes that will turn into good vehicles in which to invest. One of those is precious metals, Lutts says. He says that Cabot is not so big that it can't apply some defense strategies. "Without a doubt," Lutts says, "to be successful in this business, you have to have a strategy and discipline. Many different strategies and disciplines can work, but you have to apply them and you have to be consistent about them. And I think that's where a lot of people have failed."

Lutts says a basic fact that he learned from his dad's business is that investing is a loss discipline. "What that means is when we buy a stock, and it's high-growth, you want to be sure you're in a situation that is helping you. If you're at a point where you've lost 20 percent of your initial purchase, we simply say that we're going to sell to preserve principal. It's just a discipline. It could be 15 percent, it could be 25 percent; we use 20 percent, and it's not material what the number is. You have a plan to exit and protect the client's principal, because if you lose 50 percent of your money, you need to make 100 percent just to get it back. And that's too much; you can't be in a position where you're losing lots of your original capital or you'll just be too injured in your overall strategy."

Limiting Risk Is Important, Especially Before Big Market Drops

The 20 percent stop-loss strategy does not work as well with broad-based funds or ETFs because they are diversified, Lutts says. If you try that strategy with ETFs and the market goes down—for instance, if you sell the S&P 500 Index down 20 percent—you might be selling near the bottom. Also, if you hold an ETF because it is a fund, longer term, you will probably make a profit. Market moves are typically 10 percent, 15 percent, even 20 percent swings, Lutts says, and if you buy at a high and believe in the broad market sector, or whatever index you bought through an ETF, you should hold on for the rebound. The 20 percent rule is a risk-control tool to cut losses when trading highly dynamic stocks and especially growth stocks. "Highly dynamic growth stocks can be very volatile," Lutts says, "You can lose 80 percent of your money in those, so you need to have discipline to protect yourself."

Lutts says others have different loss disciplines. Some have an 8 percent loss discipline, which Lutts thinks is too tight and turns your system into more of a trading system. "We don't want to do that," Lutts says. "We're investors, we do our homework on a stock, we like the fundamentals, and when we put our money into it, we want to stay there for as long as possible. Hopefully it's six months or a year, two years or longer, but we fully recognize that sometimes we've made a mistake and we got it wrong and we have to protect, so that loss discipline really helps you put that plan into place." Most investors generally don't have a plan like that, Lutts says, and they don't have a strategy to limit losses, and that's what hurt investors in the last two bear markets occurring in the last decade.

When the markets go down about 50 percent and then an investor attempts to protect principal, Lutts says, that is difficult. Cabot sold a lot of its positions early in the last bear markets, let its cash build up, and started debating at what time to get back into the market. It did not know when the market would bottom, but the upside momentum started to improve, and it bought. About three months after the market bottoming it had about three-quarters of its sideline money back into the market. As far as the cash buildup in the last bear market, Lutts says, "I don't ever want to have that much cash. That's very dangerous in this business. But at certain times you just get to that position. In 28 years of being in the investment business, I don't think I'll ever relive a situation like that again."

The stop-loss strategy is for stocks and Cabot doesn't use it for ETFs. "I've studied a lot of those strategies," Lutts says, referring to ETF stop-loss strategies, "and found them very difficult. I believe that in the longer term, equities appreciate. So, the real reason to use ETFs is to allow you to get in the right areas of the market and have the best chance of appreciating. ETFs allow you to slice and dice." Lutts points out the other advantages of using ETFs: their low cost, tax efficiency, and the diversification they add. Cabot runs many of its smaller accounts, which are those in the $100,000 to $200,000 range, in strictly ETF strategies, and it tries to mimic its overall strategies in those accounts by using ETFs. "We hold ETFs for long periods of time," Lutts says, "making very small adjustments."

Bull Markets in the U.S. and Around the World

There are several bull markets in place today, Lutts believes. The first one is the emerging-markets asset class, including China, India, and Brazil. They're in a corrective phase now, he says, but longer term, they are in a very valid, bullish phase. Cabot likes a lot of the ETFs that give this asset class exposure. "What's really great today," he says, "is that there are a lot of new strategies coming out. For example, CHIQ, Global X China Consumer ETF, BRAZ, and Global X Brazil Midcap ETF are wonderful funds and give access to some very dynamic, fast-growing companies."

Lutts says that he's a basic "stock guy," and looks to find companies that have the "right drivers" behind them and the right market opportunity exposure. Having ETFs that allow access to the faster-growing global economies is a special opportunity to all people investing money today. Another ETF that Lutts likes is Van Eck Global Russia Vector (symbol RSX). "That's probably the most controversial one," he says, "and it's very cheap today." If an investor wanted exposure to emerging markets in a nonspecific target way, Lutts suggests buying an ETF such as iShares MSCI Emerging Markets ETF (symbol EEM).

Another bull market that Lutts says is in place today is the special technology area, which he calls "data-mobile." The industry is involved in giving people access to information anywhere they happen to be, and on many different types of mobile devices. This is opening up huge spending in an infrastructure segment of the Internet. There are funds and ETFs that give exposure to this sector.

There are still growth themes in the U.S., Lutts says. "The simple fact of the matter is that the U.S. runs the Internet," he says. "U.S. companies dominate the Internet. If I look out in the whole global world, I think the Internet is still in the early phases of development, and the benefits to our country and companies that lead that space are huge. So, I am investing in that part of the U.S. market fairly aggressively."

Another bull market that Lutts feels very confident about is gold and precious metals. "I think that is a very valid bull market that's in the middle phases of developing. We've gone from the denial phase into the acceptance phase," Lutts says. "What is notable is that 95 percent of the all serious money, the institutional money, has no exposure to gold."

Cabot Money Management makes the following disclosure: "Investing involves the risk of loss and past results are no guarantee of future returns. Any reference in this article to specific stocks, funds, or ETFs are meant for informational purposes only and should not be considered recommendations to buy or sell. Investment choices should be made based on thorough research in light of your time-frame, goals, and tolerance for risk."

First Affirmative Financial Network

George R. Gay, CFP, AIF (Chief Executive Officer)

www.firstaffirmative.com

First Affirmative invests in companies that contribute to a clean, healthy environment, and support a more peaceful world. Its portfolio diversification can help mitigate risks of investing in financial assets. AUM $720 million.

First Affirmative's Approach, Performing Well by Doing Good

Socially responsible investing (SRI) is hundreds of years old and its growth has accelerated since the politically active 1960s. Social investors have been involved with equality for women, civil rights, nuclear energy, and the environment, among other social concerns. It has many enthusiastic adherents, and it invests a lot of money; assets are $3.07 trillion, according the Social Investment Forum 2010 report.

For more than 20 years, First Affirmative has been a leader in sustainable and responsible investing. It produces the annual SRI in the Rockies Conference, which is the leading gathering of investors and investment professionals. The conference is aimed at helping participants direct investment capital flow in positive, healthy, and transformative ways. Creative people from all over the U.S. and the world who are passionate about the SRI industry gather to further and improve their investment methods.

First Affirmative Financial Network has been specializing in SRI, which includes sustainability, green investing, mission investing, and a full range of similar types of investing, since 1988. It became a fee-only advisor, providing investment advice for others, in 1999. First Affirmative added separate accounts and set up its own investment models, and was involved with ETFs when ETFs first began. For its small accounts, First Affirmative wanted to avoid transaction costs and used ETFs for this purpose, including the other advantages that ETFs offer.

One of the first securities that became available for First Affirmative's use was PowerShares WilderHill Clean Energy (symbol PBW), which it bought for its managed portfolios. First Affirmative monitors the worldwide ETF sources for new ETFs that fit into its investment philosophy. Recently, faith-based ETFs have been created, and First Affirmative is considering buying them for certain accounts.

George Gay, CEO of First Affirmative, says that one of the good things about ETFs is that you can see what stocks each ETF portfolio holds. ETFs are more transparent than actively managed portfolios, which might hold one stock today, and sell and hold something different next week. An ETF replicates an index, and one can look at the index and see which stocks are in the index. An active manager doesn't have this mandate and will buy and sell stocks freely, depending on the market and company outlook. So, an ETF buyer can decide whether he wants to hold a certain stock or group of stocks, because they are in a disclosed index. For example, there may be nuclear power stocks in a clean energy index, and the ETF buyer will see this and decide whether holding these stocks is an issue.

Gay says First Affirmative has never been a stock picker. It started investing with mutual funds and then brought in third-party managers to help it with portfolios. First Affirmative is also a manager-of-managers and has an increasing number of proprietary products.

First Affirmative's Commitment to Society

The ways that people deal with money—the way they spend it, save it, and invest it—affect the values and consciousness of everybody in the society, in the view of SRI investors. First Affirmative believes investors have a responsibility for the way they invest and the impact that these investments have in the world. It also believes that this consciousness can guide people into investing to help others, and it can also be a profitable way to invest.

To lessen market risk, First Affirmative uses its Sustainable Investment Solution process, which emphasizes diversification. This method guides its search to find the right mix of investments to meet its clients' investment goals. It also provides every client with an Investment Policy Statement (IPS), which details the management of the portfolio. First Affirmative portfolios are not constructed to take the risks necessary to drastically beat broad market benchmarks. Rather, its portfolio management structure is aimed at not making big mistakes, and it doesn't embrace trends that can flame out and create big losses.

Indexing blends well with the First Affirmative management style. Rather than research companies to find the most undervalued, as a bottom-up active manager would, First Affirmative concentrates on asset allocation. It periodically rebalances to keep risk proportions in line. When suggesting outside managers, it prefers to use those who use environmental, social, and governance (ESG) factors in its investment process. First Affirmative's approach is that it is a fiduciary, and the investment process, including expenses, is done in the best interests of its clients.

Investment Advice

Gay is of the opinion that investors should know what they are getting when they research and buy companies as well as ETFs. He laughs and says that unless you are a sophisticated investor, be careful with buying anything that has an X in its name, such as 2-X or 3-X. Hot stocks have recently had Xs in their names, and investing like this is reminiscent of the dot-com days, when anything with dot-com in the name went up. After that, most of the companies with dot-com in their names came crashing down. He also thinks that if you don't know what contango is, you shouldn't buy oil or other non-perishable commodity ETFs. Contango refers to the market situation where the price of a forward month futures contract is trading above the spot price of the commodity. Ordinarily futures prices of this type of commodity do trade above the spot price, but there can be differences in opinion about how high the premium should be.

Gay also says that ETF buyers should understand the implication of buying inverse ETFs, and if they don't understand, they shouldn't buy them. "Don't day trade ETFs, either, unless you are a very, very sophisticated investor," he says. "ETFs and mutual funds are intended for the retail investor to create a good asset-allocated, long-term investment plan. The fact that you can get tax benefits and cheaper expenses using ETFs still doesn't change what the average person should do, which is some amount of homework, not attempting to shoot the lights out, being able to stick with things that they understand, and avoid the rocket science trading tools designed for sophisticated traders."

As far as what to look at now, for investors who want to make basic investments for the longer term, Gay says that he likes securities, including ETFs, that give investment representation to markets that have not had much exposure. He is interested in recent funds brought out by Pax World Funds. Pax creates and manages a series of asset-allocation funds designed for investment advisors and their clients who are looking for socially responsible, green, or sustainable investments. Gay says he likes offerings such as this, and they don't have to give exposure to esoteric regions, such as "the southern corner of Africa." Gay also likes to see securities offering exposure to smaller, emerging technology industries.

Gay actively seeks out the types of investments he is looking for. He was disappointed when PowerShares dropped an ETF that was focused on efficient public transportation. This is a very narrow sector, not broad enough to gain enough investor interest, and if not enough money flows into an ETF, it is closed. He is not a stock picker, deciding what a company will do. He says, "What I want to do is to decide how much money I want to put into, for example, the solar industry. I'd rather have an ETF where I can buy the industry and not have to guess who the survivors are going to be."

For investors who want to buy and hold a portfolio of stocks, Gay thinks that ETFs are a good way to go. He says that there are ETFs that have a wide scope of asset-class exposure. When an ETF is broad in scope, such as a global ETF that also includes emerging markets, and has small-cap, mid-cap, and large-cap stocks, that is an ETF that will be fairly stable. That ETF will offer a fairly low expense ratio and will be tax-efficient. These advantages allow investors to build good quality asset-allocated portfolios that can be held for long-term growth.

Screening for Good Companies That Do Good

First Affirmative finds it's common for investors to wonder whether portfolios that use SRI strategies and use ESG principles will perform as well as portfolios that don't use these factors. It's the opinion of First Affirmative that companies that are leaders on ESG issues are companies that have innovative and forward-thinking management, and this can lead to their being leaders in their industries. This could make them good buys. One measurement that confirms this is the MSCI ESG Index, which shows that this index has outperformed the S&P 500 since the inception of the ESG Index in 1990.

In evaluating companies that are attractive to investors, screens are used to evaluate companies for their investment worth. The companies' dedication to socially responsible factors is screened to measure companies according to ESG factors. The approved companies might then be bought by SRI investors, or SRI investors might buy indexes or ETFs that contain these companies.

Analysts evaluate environmental impact by measuring variables such as carbon emissions, the amount of environmental fines, commitments to sustainability, and overall green business practices. Analysts screen companies on their human rights policies to see which companies have activities in regions where there is armed conflict or human rights abuses. Also considered are environmental justice issues, social license to operate, and product safety. The goal of social analysis is to identify companies with stronger nondiscrimination policies and better employee relations.

The culture of a company is also examined, such as what a company's policy is regarding executive pay, pay for workers, and benefits. Value gender and racial diversity on its corporate board are examined. Analysts might consider a company's legal issues, such as discrimination, fair lending, or other ethical issues.

The screens used in analyzing companies are negative or positive screens. Negative screens exclude companies that don't meet certain standards for environmental sustainability, human rights, or employee relations. Positive screens can identify the best companies in specific sectors such as renewable energy. Some funds and managers can screen out companies involved in nuclear power or animal testing, whereas others might decide to reflect different ESG priorities in their investment processes.

The MDE Group

Mitchell D. Eichen, J.D., LL.M. (Founder and CEO)
www.mdegroup.com

MDE helps clients establish personal goals and objectives and then creates diversified portfolios using a Risk First approach. This approach allocates the majority of a client's equity investments to a combination of MDE's Risk 3.0 Investment Solutions, which are core portfolio solutions adaptable to a client's unique risk tolerance and market outlook. AUM $1.35 billion.

The MDE Group Offers Its Risk First Investment Process

The MDE Group (MDE) is wondering whether investors are using the same old methods of portfolio risk management, and if so, it wants them to know it is time for a change. Despite the recent run up in the market, the 2007–2009 bear market has left an indelible scar on investors. Developing a financial plan is one story, but sticking to it during times of market distress is quite another. According to MDE, the vast majority of investors have shown that long-only, buy-and-hold investing is simply not a viable strategy. Investors seek positive returns but also reduced volatility.

MDE's Risk 3.0 portfolios aim to offer just that. By employing a Risk First investment process, Risk 3.0 portfolios are designed to provide investors with better risk-adjusted returns in difficult markets by preserving capital against small-to-moderate market losses, suffering only small declines where there are moderate market losses and substantially mitigating portfolio loss when markets fall steeply. The strategy is also designed to enhance gains in weak markets, keep pace with high, single-digit market advances, and participate—albeit at reduced levels—in double-digit market gains.

MDE believes this Risk First approach is essential for three reasons: First, after more than a decade of near-zero returns in the U.S. stock market—achieved in dramatic, zigzag fashion—many investors have lost faith in conventional methods of investment management. One of the enduring lessons of behavioral finance research is that the vast majority of individuals not only care about the end result (that is, the long-term value of their portfolios), but also the path along the way.

Second, MDE believes that investors face a new market reality defined by the combined headwinds of re-regulation, rock-bottom interest rates, continued de-leveraging, high unemployment, and slow economic growth. MDE believes these forces will result in an extended period of slow growth and persistent volatility in the markets. To address such a challenging environment, a new risk-centric paradigm is needed, one where return follows risk, not vice versa, and risk-management methods are designed to match investor risk tolerances.

Last, in these new market realities, it is MDE's opinion that preserving capital becomes even more critical to achieving long-term gains. For example, if an investment loses 15 percent, a 17.7 percent return is needed to break even; if an investment loses 25 percent, a much larger 33 percent return is needed to restore lost value; and if an investment loses 50 percent, MDE makes clear that "a whopping

100 percent return is needed to climb out of that hole." If these losses can be averted or substantially mitigated, says MDE, the investor has a much better chance of making gains overall.

Three Strategies to Preserve Capital While Maintaining Upside Participation

In 2009, MDE launched Planned Return Strategy, the first of its Risk 3.0 Investment Solutions. Planned Return Strategy is built to eliminate small-to-moderate market losses while enhancing weak-to-moderate market gains. The strategy achieves this by protecting against the first 12 percent of price decline of the S&P 500 (the "buffer"), and by multiplying market price gains by 2 times up to a cap (which is generally in the range of 8–12 percent). As a result, if the S&P 500 returns 3 percent, Planned Return Strategy will return 6 percent; if the S&P returns 5 percent, Planned Return Strategy will return 10 percent; if the S&P returns minus 10 percent, Planned Return Strategy will return 0 percent; if the S&P 500 returns minus 15 percent, Planned Return Strategy will return minus 3 percent. This is before dividends and assuming a 10 percent cap, 12 percent downside protection, and a 2x return multiplier. Returns are for a 12-month period and before fees. The actual terms depend on market conditions, and returns can vary depending on execution costs and other factors.

The second MDE strategy—Risk 3.0 Accelerated Return Strategy—is structured to enhance portfolio returns during rising markets without significantly increasing downside risk. The strategy achieves this by multiplying S&P 500 price gains by 2 times up to a cap (that is, 16–20 percent) while maintaining linear market price exposure for all market losses. Thus, if the S&P 500 returns 5 percent, Accelerated Return Strategy will return 10 percent; if the S&P returns 15 percent, Accelerated Return Strategy will return 18 percent; and if the S&P returns minus 5 percent, Accelerated Return Strategy will return minus 5 percent. This is before dividends, assuming an

18 percent cap and a return multiplier. Returns are for a 12 month period and before fees. Returns can vary, depending on execution costs and other factors.

The third strategy MDE offers is its Risk 3.0 Third Rail Strategy, which is designed to provide cost-effective protection against unpredictable market downside and extreme market shocks while retaining good upside return potential. The strategy achieves this by providing a buffer against steep market price losses from 15 to 40 percent and by retaining upside return potential up to a cap (that is, 15 percent). As a result, Third Rail Strategy has a pattern of returns such that if the S&P 500 returns 10 percent, Third Rail Strategy will return 10 percent; if the S&P returns 20 percent, Third Rail Strategy will return 15 percent; if the S&P returns minus 30 percent, Third Rail Strategy will return minus 15 percent; and if the S&P 500 returns minus 40 percent, Third Rail Strategy will return minus 15 percent. This is before dividends, assuming a 15 percent cap, downside protection between 15 percent and 40 percent, and a return multiplier. Returns are for a 12-month period and before fees. Returns may vary, depending on execution costs and other factors.

Building Investments that Provide Consistency and Predictability and No Surprises

Mitchell D. Eichen, founder and CEO of The MDE Group, says he and his team work every day to improve client satisfaction by delivering reliable results that match investor expectations. He says, "In this ever-changing world, where things are far less predictable than they were once upon a time, at the end of the day, what we're trying to bring to our clients are investments with consistency and predictability and no surprises."

In seeking to deliver this value to investors, Eichen turned to ETFs for liquidity, transparency, and low costs. But the problem with ETFs, Eichen says, is they have linear return patterns. In other words, they move up and down with their target benchmark in a one-to-one relationship.

The opposite of ETFs are hedge funds, Eichen says. Hedge funds are popular because they aim to create asymmetrical return patterns when compared to the general market and often attempt to preserve capital in down markets. But hedge funds are the exact opposite of ETFs in that they lack transparency, liquidity, and, most importantly, predictability. According to Eichen, a hedge fund might say it will deliver a certain pattern of returns, but often, it is difficult for investors to determine whether this will be the case.

"We looked at both of those separate communities," Eichen says, "and we said, 'How do we bring the best of both of those worlds together? How do we retain transparency, liquidity, and low costs, and yet provide clients with asymmetric rates of return?' What we've done is create several solutions that basically accomplish those lofty goals by marrying together ETFs and options."

Investing Risk First

Offering more background on his premise, Eichen says that most investors have been conditioned to chase returns. "When investors watch CNBC every day, read the newspapers, look on the Internet, everybody is talking about what the market is doing, and want to know if you beat your benchmark. Everybody thinks we're in some sort of competitive horse race with the market." Eichen believes an investor's true benchmark is his own personal benchmark and that an investor's objective should be to meet her goals while taking into consideration the path taken to get there.

"While most investors are focused on eking out that last dollar of return to the upside," Eichen says, "what they need to be educated on is that it is far more important to preserve capital to the downside. Once you lose money, it is very hard to recapture. We'll probably see a lot more 10 to 15 percent corrections in the months and years to come as we work through the very difficult macro environment we're facing, not only here in the U.S., but throughout the entire developed world."

MDE has coined the phrase "Risk First Investing," and Eichen says that when investors commit capital, they really should do so with risk foremost in mind, and then consider return. "We have three core portfolio strategies all based on the combination of ETFs and options," Eichen says. "We do this not in a hedge fund format, but in individually managed separate accounts in the client's name. We show daily pricing and each account has daily liquidity. Clients can see what they own."

Eichen says MDE's investment division, Risk 3.0 Asset Management, manages three distinct Risk 3.0 investment solutions: Planned Return Strategy, Accelerated Return Strategy, and Third Rail Strategy. "Each one of those solutions allows our clients to control risk on their own terms," Eichen says.

Each strategy uses a combination of options and ETFs in a series of independent slices, known as tranches. Tranches are set up to last approximately one year, and each tranche has a slightly different pattern of return based on market conditions when the tranche was placed. To receive the set pattern of return, a tranche must be held for an entire year. "If you sell the investment in the interim, it is liquid and you will get fair market pricing for it, but you will not get the for-mulaic price," Eichen says. "The reason for that is that options have embedded within them a time premium. That time premium itself does not expire until the options expire."

Because these investments last about a year, Eichen says, and MDE does not want to have to pick an inopportune time to buy or sell, MDE places one tranche per month. When each investment matures, it is rolled into a new tranche—provided MDE can place a trade with satisfactory upside caps. Caps are in large part dictated by the market's one-year implied volatility. The higher the volatility, the higher the cap MDE can return to the investor. In a choppy market,

Eichen says, the strategies do well because MDE can get great entry points to initiate positions.

In explaining how Risk 3.0 investment solutions can be adapted to individual investor risk tolerances, Eichen says they can blend a combination of the three strategies to target a desired objective. "Picture a thermostatic dial," Eichen says, "and you can dial all the way to the left if you want to protect your money, and you can dial all the way to the right if you want to power up your money and get a more aggressive return. And the dial can be placed for someone who wants to be in the middle, who wants to get consistent, decent returns and yet protect downside risk."

Alesco Advisors, LLC

James G. Gould, CPA (President) www.alescoadvisors.com

Alesco focuses its investment process on asset allocation, which it believes is the primary driver of investment returns. Alesco analyzes and then invests with a concentration on asset classes, weightings, diversification, and rebalancing. AUM $1.4 billion.

Asset Allocation Specialists for Each Client

Alesco Advisors believes that the primary factor of investment returns is asset allocation and strives to customize client portfolios by having the right asset class weightings in its portfolios. Alesco analyzes various asset classes to obtain optimal diversification and rebalances portfolios on an ongoing basis. Its investment philosophy is based on the conclusions of academic and industry studies. As a result, Alesco rarely uses active investment managers. Instead it utilizes passively managed index-based securities such as ETFs and mutual funds. In this way, it believes it can eliminate or minimize commonly made investment mistakes and focus its efforts on proper asset allocation, broad diversification, and keeping costs low.

It refers to this approach as "Intelligent Investing," and bases much of its asset-allocation modeling on academic research and empirical studies. Alesco develops asset-allocation strategies that seek to capture the return of the capital markets and reduce risk. It has a flexible approach that allows it to construct portfolios for each client, knowing that one strategy is not right for everyone. It works with both institutional and individual clients as a discretionary manager, but also acts as an investment consultant on a nondiscretionary basis. Alesco is an independent, fee-based manager, working for the client and offering investment solutions and superior service for those who recognize the benefits of its philosophy.

Alesco offers its broadly diversified Global Balanced Portfolio to financial professionals and clients of these professionals. The portfolio holds between 12 and 20 ETFs to gain broad diversification and is designed to produce long-term appreciation through dynamic beta strategies while employing carefully selected, risk-controlled tactical allocation trades.

Alesco Started Using ETFs About When ETFs Were Born

James Gould, president of Alesco Advisors, says that the firm was designed coming out of the late 1990s, when there was a massive migration out of value investing and moving into growth, especially into large-cap growth and ultimately into technology bubble stocks. Gould, at this time, was president of a small-cap to mid-cap value equity firm and says he realized so many people were making bad decisions by piling into large-cap growth stocks. "They were not really understanding what was going to be happening to them," Gould says, "even though we were warning them all along the way."

Gould says that in 1999, he met a mutual fund consultant who was very well versed in mutual funds, and he explained ETFs to Gould. "I knew a little bit about them," Gould says, "I had heard of the SPDRs, the Qs, the Diamonds, but the offerings were very limited in terms of what asset classes were available." The consultant said that a broader offering was coming and that iShares were being created that would significantly enhance the ETF market. Alesco Advisors got started from this development. Gould figured there was a better way for his clients to get a broad level of diversification. Alesco started modestly, "With zero assets and a rolodex. Little did we know, in January 2000," Gould says, "that within just a few months, the bubble would burst and people would begin to 'get religion' as to the benefits of broad-based asset allocation and diversification."

In the summer of 2000, a number of new iShares ETFs were introduced, very much expanding the universe of choices for asset classes in the ETF marketplace. Gould says Alesco is not an ETF-only manager, but uses primarily index-based investment vehicles to build client portfolios. Gould says, "Philosophically speaking, that comes from not just my own personal beliefs but also from many academic studies that show active managers have a tendency to underperform their benchmarks, particularly net of fees. In addition, there's also very much an asymmetric characteristic of their performances in that the absolute amount of active-manager underperformance has a tendency to be substantially more than the absolute amount of their outperformance." Because of this, Gould says that on a risk-adjusted basis, owning the asset class via an index-based investment makes a lot more sense than investing with an active manager.

Asset Allocation and Style Purity, Drivers of Portfolio Performance

There is also the benefit of style purity when you hold an index-based investment versus investing with a manager, Gould says. In the late 1990s, he points out the biggest names in value investing drifted in style and moved over to the growth side, giving in to the pressures of their clients' demanding better results. This changed the risk profiles of client portfolios. So, in the early 2000s, at a time when clients needed their value managers to be the most style-pure, they were the least style-pure. When growth stock valuations collapsed and the dot-com market broke down, many value managers participated in the market meltdown. Using index-based investments and a passive investment strategy ensures style purity and is a major benefit to Alesco's clients, Gould says.

Style drift can affect the ability to control risk in portfolios. Gould sees style drift as a significant negative characteristic of active management. For example, when value managers drift into growth stocks, or domestic managers drift into international stocks, or large-cap managers buy small-cap stocks, the portfolio no longer has the risk profile the advisor originally anticipated. Gould says, "When you buy a passive index-based investment, such as when you buy a domestic large-cap value index fund, whether it's a mutual fund or an ETF, all you're going to have in that investment is domestic large-cap value companies. However, should you put your money with a domestic large-cap value equity actively managed fund, that money manager can look at value differently, define it differently than the traditional metrics of the industry, or just make a conscious effort to move away from the primary investment style thinking that they can increase returns or reduce risk by going into other parts of the market."

Gould says portfolio performance is about developing the right asset allocation for each client. He says there are studies that show that more than 90 percent of a portfolio's return is attributable to asset allocation, and the balance of the return is attributable to cost, as well as the value added or subtracted from the results of security selection. He prefers building portfolios by picking asset classes instead of stock picking. Gould argues that using stock picking is not rational. After all, if one puts in a lot of time and effort to build a portfolio with the risk profile that is appropriate for the client, all that effort can be offset by a manager that does not stick to its knitting, which is style drift, or a manager with chronically below-market investment results.

The other big advantage in index-based investing, Gould says, is that you eliminate manager risk. There are all kinds of manager risk. For instance, a manager might sell his business, receive a lot of money, and not work as hard as when he owned the company. Another example is that in stock picking management firms, the analysts who picked the stocks to create the great track record may have been hired away by another manager, or retired, or started his own firm. The replacement analyst might not be nearly as good, and performance will suffer. This type of risk goes away when a portfolio is constructed using index-based investments.

Alesco Advisor's Asset-Class Strategy

Alesco is a broad-based asset-allocation firm. Gould says, "We view ourselves as a global manager, we allocate money across all the major asset classes, we are indifferent to style as defined by value, growth, or momentum, and we are indifferent as to market capitalization. Asset classes have personalities, and have risk-return profiles that if looked at over longer periods of time are quite consistent. For example, in domestic equities, micro-cap stocks have by far the best long-term average performance; however, they also have by far the highest level of volatility." Other asset classes, Gould finds, also have consistent, long-term risk profiles.

"What we have done," Gould says, "is modeled various iterations of asset classes mixes to come up with what we believe is the most attractive risk-adjusted profile for an all-equity portfolio, and we have done similar work for fixed income. Then it becomes getting the right fixed-income and equity blend for each client based on their objectives." As far as Alesco Advisors' fixed-income universe, Gould says that they work with institutional and high-net worth clients. Institutional clients often have different needs from the fixed-income component of their portfolios than individuals do.

High-net worth client portfolios typically hold municipal bonds. Which bonds to buy depends on the state in which the client resides. Because of the varying levels of risk in bonds of different states, Alesco diversifies the risk and often buys bonds outside of clients' home state. For institutional clients, Alesco usually goes to its default position, which is buying a broad-bond market ETF. There are times, Gould says, when different parts of the bond market—it could be mortgage-backed securities, it could be corporates, it could be Treasuries—look more or less attractive, relative to their own historic valuation characteristics and also relative to other parts of the bond market.

As these valuation characteristics move more or less favorably for one of the different bond market parts, Alesco might over-weight or under-weight specific areas of the bond market. Alesco's intent is to own more of the cheaper parts and less of the more expensive parts of the bond market. This is much the same as what Alesco attempts to do in the stock market.

As far as fixed-income pricing at the time of their analysis in 2011, Gould says U.S. Agency Bonds and Treasury Bonds are expensive relative to their historical valuation measures. Mortgage-backed securities are the cheapest part of the bond market. Investment-grade corporate bonds are pretty much in line with their historic spreads relative to Treasury Bonds. High-yield bonds have small premiums to their historical valuations. Gould says that an interesting area is floating-rate bank loans. Floating-rate bank loans are inexpensive and are also attractive because of their short duration. These securities are LIBOR-based floating-rate instruments and, therefore, as interest rates move up, the yield moves up. The change in LIBOR and the change in the yield of the investment are not in lock step; there is a lag, but the securities perform better than longer-duration bonds in a rising-rate environment. Interestingly, the floating-rate investment we use is actually one of the few actively managed investments in our portfolio," Gould says.

Alesco Advisors segregates its portfolios into three different components. "We have an equity component, we have a traditional fixed-income component, and then we have real-return assets," Gould says. "The real-return assets often include Treasury Inflation Protected

Securities, REITs, both domestic and international, and may include commodity and/or currency funds" he says, adding, "Alesco's credo is to keep things simple. Wall Street makes things more complicated than is necessary. Our investment methodology is straightforward, low-cost, and transparent."

Navellier & Associates

Louis G. Navellier (Founder and Chairman)

www.navellier.com

Navellier's research is focused on finding and exploiting inefficiencies in the market, and its disciplined quantitative analysis system attempts to outperform the market over the long term, which is at least five years. Navellier builds varied domestic and international portfolios. AUM $2.8 billion.

Navellier Offers Investment Strategies in Several Areas

Navellier Associates constructs portfolios that are based on its investment process that uses controlled risk while seeking high returns. It builds long-term relationships with clients and consultants through its regular market commentaries, portfolio updates, and a number of products and services, using several asset classes, including ETFs.

Navellier Associates' portfolios are domestic and international, and spread across capitalization weights, and are constructed using various formulas. The methods used include stock picking, index replicating, index enhancing, and ETF long and short absolute strategies. The stock portfolios seek to identify fundamentally superior stocks that are on track for strong and sustainable growth. Navellier Associate's team of professionals is available to help investors through its disciplined quantitative process.

One of the areas in which Navellier Associates focuses is growth investing, in which it seeks out vital, growing companies. It believes that finding companies that push the economy forward is a potent, wealth-building strategy. To find these companies, it uses a combination of quantitative and fundamental analysis, and from this, its team of analysts develops a list of stock buy recommendations weekly.

Whether analyzing companies or ETFs, Navellier Associates uses fundamental analysis. It favors companies that increase sales, because it thinks sales numbers are hard to fake. It also likes companies that have a good cash flow and a history of positive earnings. It seeks growth stocks that show buying pressure, thinking that those stocks can continue upward momentum.

It looks for companies that have expanding operating margins, which tells them whether earnings are growing faster than sales. Usually these companies are dominant in their industries and can raise prices without experiencing a drop in sales. Navellier Associates favors companies that show consistent growth in its earnings and also likes stocks that have earnings estimates revised upwards by analysts. They want to see a growing rate of growth increase. Earnings surprises on the upside is another indicator and tells them that perhaps analysts aren't following the company closely yet and it might be a sleeper.

A large and growing free cash flow number is positive and tells how much a company has left over after paying for its costs of doing business. Also important is a company's return on equity, which tips off how efficiently a company manages its resources.

Ways to Use ETFs

Louis Navellier, founder and chairman, points out that some ETFs are thinly traded, so you have to know what you're doing, and if you place a market order, you are at the mercy of the specialist. For this reason, some investors and traders deal in the more liquid ETFs. ETFs are ideal for hedging. Navellier says, "In the old days, if you wanted to protect a portfolio, you could buy put options, but you always had to pay a premium. There are no premiums with inverse ETFs, and if the market goes down, you get rewarded right away."

Another time that ETFs are especially useful is when the market is coming out of a really bad cycle, such as the 2008 crash. Louis Navellier says managers can't buy what had become such low-quality securities because they could be sued for dealing in questionable equities. But you can buy an ETF that contains these stocks, and as low-quality stocks in the index climb, so will the ETF. As the market moves away from a crash, the market goes to quality, Louis Navellier says, because there are short squeezes, forcing low-quality stocks higher.

Navellier's Long and Short ETF Offering

Navellier Associates offers its Global Macro Allocation Portfolio (GMAP), an actively managed portfolio of ETFs that was developed to outperform in advancing and declining markets. The portfolio contains long and inverse ETFs and attempts to have lower volatility while outperforming.

Louis Navellier says, "We recommend some sector ETFs in our newsletters because they often break out before the stocks break out, and we have an ETF grader on Navellier.com where we rank them. When we put together an ETF portfolio, it was extremely hard to beat the market, and the only product we came up with was our Global Macro Allocation Portfolio." After researching, the Navellier portfolio managers, Michael Garaventa and Tim Hope, gathered and tested a list of ETFs that were suitable for the portfolio. Louis Navellier says, "With ETFs, you can short real estate, you can do all kinds of neat things, and then we did an inverse ETF overlay because of the flash crash of 2010, and the inverse ETF overlay is tied to the VIX volatility." The CBOE Volatility Index is commonly referred to as the VIX. Traders call it the "fear index," because it does show how afraid traders and investors are. As markets drop, volatility almost always goes up, and the VIX climbs.

Louis Navellier likes GMAP largely because it moves so opposite of the market. Rather than short-selling shares or an ETF to establish a position, an investor or trader can merely buy an inverse ETF. The portfolio has been back-tested and is now ready to trade.

Blending and Optimizing Portfolios

At its latest posting, GMAP holds only about 16 ETFs, consisting of 10 long positions and 6 short positions. They utilize various momentum models in their modeling, according to the portfolio co-manager, Tim Hope. "I think a good way to describe it," Hope says, "is to have the markets communicate to us what's working or not. A way to envision it, particularly given that we have these inverse ETFs, is to look at the market as an ocean, and that an ocean has waves. The market and different asset classes come in and out of favor, as the waves of the ocean come in and out. That's what we're utilizing in terms of what the market is communicating to us in certain asset classes." When the market starts performing well, Hope says they begin to start "sliding into" the ETFs that look promising. The asset classes that look weak and give indications of downside momentum are the ones in which they will buy inverse ETFs for participation on the short side.

Garaventa and Hope aren't making forward-looking fundamental decisions on asset classes, such as deciding that gold will go higher or that emerging markets are the asset class to buy for the next year. Rather, they analyze what the markets and various classes tell them and they invest accordingly.

Louis Navellier says that the GMAP portfolio is based on a different cycle than stocks. The Navellier Associates Stock Grader, which is online at Navellier.com, uses a 52-week cycle, longer than the GMAP cycle. Louis Navellier says ETFs move much more differently than the underlying market and says that they use un-leveraged ETFs and mostly plain ETFs, and are "trying to stay away from all the kinky stuff." As for time periods, Hope says, "We're trying to utilize those time periods of 30, 60, and 90 days to pick up on that weighting in terms of what's working in the market."

ETFs Are Effective for Long and Short Positions

Navellier Associates recommends sectors in its newsletter and posts early warning alerts for sector ETFs. Investors can also go to navallier.com and to the ETF Grader to check recommendations. Investors can see whether the ETFs they hold rank well, and if they are not an A or a B, which is a strong buy or a buy, Navellier Associates doesn't recommend their being bought or held.

Navellier's portfolio managers constantly attempt to optimize and to blend portfolios, and ETFs help them accomplish this goal. "The beauty of the inverse ETF," Louis Navellier says, "is we can do a better job of optimizing blending than we can with stocks only. Our optimization models are designed to get the highest return with the least amount of risk, so when you throw anything into our optimization model, you find something called the "tangent," which is the optimal trade-off. And then you can throttle up or down and make it more aggressive or conservative. So, when we find the tangent in stocks, you're going to have 10 to 12 percent a year of volatility, based on standard deviation. And you're going to have a much higher beta. Our beta is usually at or near 1. When you do the ETF Global Macro Allocation Portfolio, the deviation is far lower and the betas are extremely low."

ETFs almost figure as another asset class for Navellier Associates and give them the ability to efficiently go short. ETFs hold a stock portfolio, and if you buy an inverse ETF, you are shorting the same stocks in that portfolio. Shorts are opposite of the long positions in the GMAP portfolio, "and that is the beauty of it," Louis Navellier says. "So, if I try to put an inverse ETF overlay on some of my stock positions, which I do, and we tie it to the VIX volatility, it's not a perfect match. In the ETF world, it is a perfect match."

Using VIX for Long and Short Strategies

As far as how big a long and short position to take, Hope says his team uses a variation of the VIX to determine positions and lets the fear element dictate how big a short position to take. If VIX goes up, GMAP will be larger on the short side. Another factor that stands out for GMAP is the team's discipline, which makes possible its ability to execute its strategies. Hope says that this is an important factor because an individual might have the same strategy but might start to doubt the strategy or might not be able to trade as successfully as his seasoned team.

Analyzing and using VIX is an important element in gauging market sentiment. "Let me say something about the flash crash, and I know they've tried putting in uniform circuit breakers so it doesn't happen again," Louis Navellier says, referring to the inter-day crash of May 6, 2010. "About three weeks prior to the flash crash, we had record low VIX volatility, and then suddenly we had very high volatility. We all looked at it and said, 'Oh, my God, what are we going to do, what if this happens again?' That flash crash apparently came out of Waddell & Reed on a futures transaction, and they executed the same trade four days later and it was fine. It looks like they just hit the market at a bad time of the day and the New York Stock Exchange breakers went off."

Louis Navellier says the exchanges have since installed uniform circuit breakers, which should help. He also notes that the VIX volatility has been low for a while, and points out that the high-frequency traders have disappeared from the market, which might account for some of the lower volatility. Volatility is not going away, as Louis Navellier says, "We know there are times of the year when it's going to be volatile."

RiverFront Investment Group

Michael Jones, CFA (Founding Partner, Chairman, and CIO) www.riverfrontig.com

RiverFront stays in constant communication with its clients regarding its thought processes, decisions, and even its mistakes. Its team of seasoned investment professionals works to deliver returns without taking undue risk through a global, tactical, asset-allocation strategy. AUM $3 billion.

RiverFront Seeks to Combine Value with Momentum

RiverFront believes that on a long-term basis, markets price assets according to fundamentals, so its long-term, asset-allocation strategy is driven by the search for value. It believes that the buying price of an asset class is the most important item determining an investor's return. However, on a short-to-medium term basis, markets act like voting machines, pricing assets according to many factors, including popularity. Because of this, RiverFront's strategies combine both value and momentum factors.

When fashioning its long-term allocation strategy, RiverFront emphasizes asset classes that trade below average prices relative to the historical norm. Its long-term strategy is then modified with tactical tilts designed to blend with current market trends, which increases the weighting of asset classes that experience positive momentum. In this way, its asset-allocation strategy combines RiverFront's judgment of value with its sense of momentum, and when its evaluation of value and momentum are aligned, it makes its biggest investments.

RiverFront's investment process is a multilayered investment discipline, which starts with its time-proven method of strategic asset allocation. It then continues with tactical allocation, sector strategy, and optimized security selection. It continues the process using its proven disciplined risk-management program, which it has developed and used for many years. RiverFront believes that its process ensures that portfolio performance does not rely on the success of any one set of decisions and executes simultaneously all of the layers of its discipline. It has found that its portfolios have provided consistently superior performance as different layers in the process have added value at different times.

RiverFront's Investment Processes

RiverFront Investment Group is the former advice, strategy, and portfolio-management department for Wachovia Securities. Michael Jones was the former CIO for Wachovia and is now the CIO at River-Front. Jones and a group of associates left Wachovia in 2008 to form an independent money manager, and Wachovia granted them rights to the track record of the portfolios they had managed. RiverFront is built around the historical track record of the global tactical allocation concept that this group pioneered at Wachovia.

Jones says, "What we build our portfolios around is the notion that asset allocation is not a static proposition. We determine about how much risk we are willing to take in a portfolio, and then go around the world looking for the two elements that we look for in an investment: value and momentum." Jones has a broad definition of value and says that value is any asset class, including stocks, bonds, currencies, commodities, and any other asset class that sells at a great price relative to its long-term history.

RiverFront builds mathematical models that relate pricing levels to future returns, and Jones says that these models keep telling him something that everyone intuitively knows but has a hard time implementing in their portfolios: low prices are good. He says, "You get above-average returns, historically, when you pay below-average prices. So the first thing we want to do is focus on value and build an asset-allocation strategy that puts more of the portfolio in the cheapest asset classes all around the world. But we have discovered something in 25 years of investing that persuades us to not exclusively rely on value, and that is that cheap asset classes often get cheaper, and expensive asset classes continue rising much higher than you think they could possibly rise."

Because of these factors, RiverFront combines the value discipline with a momentum process. The momentum process uses technical analysis that tries to hold back its portfolio managers from catching what Jones calls a "falling knife," and the managers wait until the market signals that the asset class has bottomed and is safe to buy. Or, if the portfolio managers are already holding an asset, Jones says that the momentum process "holds us back from selling that rocket ship asset class that's ridiculously overvalued." He thinks that gold is a good example of an asset class that has moved very high, exceeding expectations for many investors.

But even though an asset class appears high, RiverFront holds it until the market signals that the asset class is losing its upward momentum and that the asset class is "ready to return to Earth." Jones says that his team tries to make sure the biggest allocations are in asset classes where value and momentum are aligned, where the asset class is cheap as far as value and is priced cheaply by the market.

The ETF Revolution Creating a New World of Investing

As far as asset classes used by RiverFront, in the equities, it uses large-cap, mid-cap, and small-cap stocks, emerging markets, emerging markets small-cap, developed international, and developed international small-cap. It also uses investment grade bonds, high-yield bonds, foreign currencies, commodities, and other asset classes. Jones says that the ETF revolution has been powerful for RiverFront's style of investing, and without it, RiverFront could not have gone down its present investment path.

ETFs combine hundreds of individual stocks or bonds into a single investment security. Before the ETF revolution, an appropriately diversified portfolio had to have at least 30 to 40 stocks in every country in which it invested. Given the large number of countries and asset classes in RiverFront portfolios, without ETFs, its portfolios would have to hold at least 300 to 400 different securities. With ETFs, he says, "Suddenly we can put 3 percent of the portfolio in Latin America and know that we have broad diversification across all of the countries and all of the stocks within that region even though we only purchased single ETF securities. The ETF eliminates individual stock risk, and the only risk we have is that we make a mistake about where value existed in the marketplace." He thinks that the evolution of ETFs was the enabling technology that enabled River-Front to grow and evolve.

RiverFront Portfolios Built for Different Objectives

RiverFront offers asset allocation for investors seeking conservative, moderate, long-term growth, and moderate growth and income portfolios. It offers ETF portfolios for conservative, moderate, and long-term growth goals, and portfolios constructed for foundations, consisting of large-cap and small-to-mid-cap equities designed to complement almost any allocation mix.

Jones says that he wishes his portfolio managers could perfectly time the market, shifting all of the money out of stocks at the right time and putting it into bonds, and then reversing the trade at precisely the right moment. But of course, it is pretty much impossible to do that all of the time. RiverFront lets the client set her long-term investment return and choose the best portfolio for her target. River-Front's Value and Momentum disciplines the portfolio managers to add or subtract from that baseline risk level as their assessments of market conditions dictate.

Each RiverFront portfolio balances investment need and risk tolerance differently based upon a specific time horizon. Jones has a patent pending on an optimization process that optimizes across the portfolio based upon a 3-, 5-, 7-, or 10-year investment time frame.

The client can select the RiverFront portfolio that matches his risk tolerance and investment objectives. For instance, the client might say that he has about a 5-year investment time frame, which according to RiverFront equates over the long term to about 50 percent stocks and 50 percent bonds. Or, he could say he has at least a 10-year investment horizon, which equates in RiverFront's framework to 100 percent high risk, high volatility, and maximum growth assets. Or, a client might want to be somewhere in the middle between these two. RiverFront sets the broad risk parameters for each portfolio and varies a portfolio significantly due to changing market conditions.

As an example of portfolio variance, Jones says that RiverFront's most popular portfolio, the Moderate Growth & Income Portfolio, is targeted to a 5-year horizon and typically has about a 50 percent mix of stocks and bonds. Early in 2009, The Moderate Growth & Income Portfolio had approximately 25 percent in stocks and 75 percent in cash, bonds, and a small amount in an alternative investment. Four months later, it had 75 percent in stocks, commodities, and high-yield bonds. For the year 2009, the portfolio was up 24 percent. "What we want to be is awesome risk managers, protect your downside, and increase and amplify your upside," Jones says.

A New and Improved Way to Build Optimal Portfolios

"Our optimization process," Jones says, "is proprietary, and is at historical ranges of returns for various asset classes, based upon the price you're paying right now." RiverFront has 140 years of stock data and looks at every period of history that started at about the current valuation levels. It analyzes the best-case historical outcome starting from current prices, the worst case, and the average return. This analysis reveals the powerful impact the starting price has on potential returns. As an example, RiverFront personnel identified in 1999 that large-cap stocks were so overvalued that, according to historical data, investors were almost certain to lose money over the coming decade.

This impact of price on subsequent return is based upon "mean reversion," a concept in which assets with above-average prices tend to decline over time, whereas under-priced assets tend to rise. However, it takes time for these mean reversion tendencies of markets to assert themselves, RiverFront says. Thus, the longer the investment horizon, the more mean reversion has time to affect investor returns.

Because mean reversion has an increasing impact the longer the investment time frame, RiverFront analyzes potential upside, downside, and average returns over a 3-, 5-, 7-, and a 10-year period of time. RiverFront does this analysis for every asset class and for downside risk analysis, RiverFront assumes that risky assets decline together.

RiverFront's optimization process builds a portfolio that offers the most upside potential consistent with an extremely high probability of making money by a certain horizon date even in a worst-case scenario. Portfolios are constructed that should make money at 3-, 5-, 7-, and 10-year time horizons. Longer investment horizons give more time for mean reversion to take hold, and therefore portfolios with those longer investment time frames tend to have much higher allocations to higher volatility asset classes whose prices suggest a high probability of making money if given sufficient time.

Currencies and Commodities

In that framework, at the present time, RiverFront's portfolios have about a 7 percent allocation to foreign currencies. Its optimization discipline says that foreign currencies have better yields than domestic bonds, and their volatility is only slightly higher than domestic bonds. RiverFront sees this as a value opportunity and a momentum opportunity for its clients.

Wisehaupt Bray Asset Management at HighTower Advisors

David Wisehaupt (Managing Director and Chief Investment Strategist) www.hightoweradvisors.com

The portfolio management team's operating philosophy is to always put the interest of its clients first. The team believes the best way to do that is through a disciplined, well thought-out and well-executed investment process that incorporates both a top-down and bottom-up approach. AUM in excess of $3 billion.

A Tale of Two Investment Styles

Wisehaupt Bray Asset Management (WBAM) at HighTower Advisors combines both top-down and bottom-up methods to build risk-adjusted portfolios designed to meet the investment needs and objectives of each individual client. The portfolios can "go anywhere," meaning they can invest in equities, fixed income, currencies, and other asset classes. They also can take short positions using inverse ETFs.

David Wisehaupt, managing director and CIO, and Stella Bray, portfolio manager, believe in using risk-reduction techniques such as sell stops to protect capital and enhance long-term portfolio performance. Investment objectives depend on the specific needs of individual clients, but the process aims to give every client the opportunity for stronger risk-adjusted performance. The goal is to deliver greater long-term returns than the investor would receive by taking the same risk level using indexes.

WBAM follows its investment discipline rigorously and believes the most important type of diversification is achieved through a variety of investment styles. Consequently, its equity-investing decisions are split equally between two methods.

Half the stocks in a client's equity portfolio are selected using a top-down approach. WBAM begins by studying macro-economic trends and quantitative factors and performing technical analysis at the sector level. After the sectors have been selected, the firm uses quantitative and technical research to identify every publicly traded company within those industries that may meet its investment criteria for a particular client. Additional research and analysis trim the list down to about 20 stocks. If the process does not identify 20 appropriate stocks, WBAM holds a portion of the portfolio in cash or adds to fixed income, currency, or precious metal positions, and it might invest in ETFs.

The other half of the equity portfolio is selected using the bottom-up process, which starts with examining more than 2,000 securities. According to Wisehaupt, earnings estimate revisions are an important clue to the future direction of a stock price. Companies whose earnings estimates have been raised two or more times in a short period of time are analyzed using both fundamental and technical research. The firm looks for 18 companies to place in this half of the portfolio. Again, if 18 appropriate stocks are not found, WBAM might hold a portion of the portfolio in cash, add to fixed income, currency, or precious metal holdings, or use ETFs.

The same stocks are owned in all client portfolios, but they are in different proportions based on a client's specific risk-tolerance and investment goals.

For the fixed-income portion of a client's portfolio, investments are selected using an interest rate anticipator approach, which seeks to maximize the return on the bond portfolio by forecasting interest-rate trends and establishing an average term to maturity. Depending on a client's needs, fixed-income investments are taxable or tax-free. Typically, WBAM invests in individual debt issues, investment-grade bonds, or ETFs.

According to Wisehaupt, the firm has a two-pronged sell discipline. In the bottom-up portion of the portfolio, each equity position is assigned a sell stop price. Sell stops are raised when deemed appropriate but never lowered. The margin between the stop price and the market price differ from stock to stock and, on the same stock, at different stages in its growth cycle. In some instances, the managers assign stop prices to stage out of a position. In others, they set stops to sell the entire position at one time. In the bottom-up half of the portfolio, a lower earnings revision usually results in the sale of the stock.

Facing a "Fork in the Road"

Before joining HighTower in December 2008, Wisehaupt was at Merrill Lynch for more than 26 years. When Merrill was acquired by Bank of America in 2008, Wisehaupt came to the conclusion that the new culture and way of doing business at BoA-Merrill was not compatible with his long-standing approach to serving clients.

After an exhaustive search, he settled on HighTower, an advisor-owned firm focused on the needs of individual and institutional investors. According to Wisehaupt, HighTower was the one firm he found that operated as close to the way he would do business if he opened his own firm.

In Wisehaupt's view, every investor falls into two categories: those who believe it is impossible to beat the market over the long term and those who believe it is possible to beat the market over the long term. The first group should rely on an asset-allocation strategy. Its portfolios will be allocated to different asset classes, rebalanced periodically, and fully invested all the time.

For the second group, beating the market on a risk-adjusted basis over the long term requires a methodical and process-driven approach. Wisehaupt has researched different ways an investor can accomplish this objective. One that he particularly likes is an ETF strategy based on a 2004 study by Ibbotston Associates ("Highlights from Case Study on BXM Buy-Write Options Strategy").

The strategy assumes an investor buys the S&P 500 Index, holds it, and writes covered calls against it. According to the study, the advantage of this buy-write strategy "is that the option premium received cushions downside moves in an equity portfolio."

Overall, WBAM believes one of the best things the firm can do for its clients—no matter which group of investors they fall into—is make decisions about which market sectors represent the "sweet spot" for investments.

Wisehaupt says, "We don't necessarily want to be invested in all parts of the stock market at all times. If we can do things that are a little smarter and use a well thought-out process, over time we're hopeful we can select and invest in market sectors that will outperform and avoid those that underperform."

Using ETFs and Writing Covered Calls to Improve Performance

WBAM attempts to keep its buy-write strategy as close as possible to the Ibbotson study, which was done on the entire market, used covered call-writing against the S&P 500 index, and did not use individual stocks. Although WBAM does not want to inject the risk of owning individual stocks into client portfolios, it does attempt to improve on the process by including sector picks.

According to Wisehaupt, WBAM uses a "weight of the evidence approach" when deciding which industry sectors to buy and which to avoid. The firm looks at macro-economic trends, such as leading indicators, performs quantitative research to determine which sectors of the economy are experiencing growing profits, and analyzes the return on equity of the various sectors. The firm performs technical analysis, both on the broad market and individual sectors.

Wisehauapt says WBAM uses various ETFs at different times because the firm makes bets not only on sectors but also industries. The firm prefers unmanaged, rather than managed, ETFs and selects mostly from the iShares series. However, according to Wisehaupt, WBAM uses equal-weighted, fundamentally weighted, or any series of ETFs it thinks is appropriate in a given market environment.

For instance, Wisehaupt says when WBAM saw opportunity in the commodity space, it bought ETFs that had commodity exposures. It used gold and silver ETFs and sold calls when those asset classes looked attractive.

WBAM has avoided sectors including REITs and financials. According to Wisehaupt, the firm's risk aversion, combined with its top-down analysis, kept it out of real estate and financial when those sectors imploded in 2008.

"We looked at the buying that was taking place in real estate and saw situations where people were buying for little or no money down and paying interest-only loans in many cases," recalls Wisehaupt. "So we asked ourselves, are these people really buyers? They looked to us more like renters. We asked ourselves further, if they are renters, who are the real buyers, who are the owners of the property?

"The conclusion we came to was that the banks were the real owners and we didn't believe that banks are all that good at being owners of real estate. Their business model is different and they typically are not able to operate real estate well due to the regulatory structure of the banking industry."

Although WBAM has not been in real estate or financials for several years, Wisehaupt does not rule them out for the future.

Buying Mostly U.S. Bonds for the Present

In addition to ETF portfolios, WBAM manages combinations of stock and bond holdings, depending on clients' needs. Those portfolios consist of individual equities and debt issues.

On the fixed-income side, the firm invests in and manages taxable and tax-free bonds, based on the client's tax situation. WBAM also manages balanced portfolios of individual stocks and bonds. These portfolios are process-driven and do not use ETFs. The same methodology of half top-down/half bottom-up is used for equity investing in these portfolios.

On the fixed-income side of these portfolios, WBAM sticks to its interest rate anticipator approach, which allows the firm to buy positions for its taxable and tax-free bond portfolios based on its view of the direction interest rates are heading.

WBAM also uses ETFs in its fixed-income portfolios to complement individual bond holdings. The firm has invested primarily in domestic corporate bonds for its clients' fixed-income portfolios because, according to Wisehaupt, differences in accounting standards outside the U.S. pose a potential risk factor. He says WBAM can buy foreign bonds in the future as better data becomes available and transparency increases.

"I suspect we will do more international investing in bonds than we currently do," Wisehaupt said. "At present, we believe investors are better off investing in U.S. fixed income and the risk/return metrics bear that out."

CLS Investments, LLC

Todd Clarke (President) www.clsinvest.com

CLS believes that risk budgeting is the core to its risk planning and delivering returns to customer portfolios. Risk budgeting is based on customer financial goals, capability to handle risk, and time horizon. Risk budgeting aids in monitoring risk. AUM $ 7.5 billion.

CLS Emphasizes Client Risk Budgeting

CLS Investments (CLS) considers risk budgeting integral to its execution of portfolio management. CLS advisors work with each client to determine the risk budget, and base it on each client's ability to handle risk, time horizon, and financial goals. CLS determines a client's comfort zone and regulates his portfolio so that he is comfortable in his investment posture. The level of risk managed by the risk budget is set in place by CLS after consulting with the client. A client risk budget is assigned, and that risk cannot be overspent or under-used, and as the growth posture is pursued, portfolio managers keep the risk level consistent.

Many investors believe that bonds have less risk than stocks, and that bonds are conservative and stocks are aggressive asset classes. Through its risk-budgeting methodology, CLS understands that risk actually moves on a continuum and that some stocks contain less risk than some bonds, and some bonds contain more risk than stocks. CLS makes portfolio adjustments based on asset classes according to the client's risk budget. This allows CLS to over-weight growth areas when appropriate and under-weight underperforming asset classes when needed.

Risk-budgeting considerations are central to CLS's portfolio weightings. The company has found that the risk level of stocks varies greatly between stock issues and also between different bond issues. There can also be great differences in volatility in mutual funds, even those in the same asset class. For this reason, portfolios are actively managed and portfolio risk is controlled by counter-balancing trades. Market timing and other technical asset allocation are not used, but performance is sought by over-weighting promising asset classes. CLS seeks to capitalize on promising sectors of the market by using its core and satellite methodology.

CLS has determined that as the risk levels of asset classes drift over time, market conditions change. CLS's team tracks market movements and makes adjustments to client portfolios to match each portfolio's risk-budgeting target. CLS makes adjustments to other holdings in each portfolio to keep portfolios on track.

Through its innovative solutions, CLS can deliver risk budgeting to a wide variety of investors. CLS combines an individualized risk budget with each investment plan that is constructed to fit each CLS investor.

Investing with Risk Very Much in Mind

CLS is in a unique spot, says Todd Clarke, president of the firm, in the sense that it is in the middle ground between passive and active management. "We believe in asset allocation and diversifying our clients' portfolios, but we do over-weight and under-weight areas to take advantage of the areas that are growing," Clarke says.

The yearly portfolio turnover for CLS is about 40 percent, so Clarke says an active manager would call CLS passive, and a passive manager would call it active, and that's the way it fits in the middle ground. CLS follows its risk-budgeting philosophy, which means that each of its clients is assigned a level of risk. The level works like a budget in that the client can spend only so much risk in a portfolio. When CLS makes portfolio adjustments—for example, when it over-weights growth, under-weights bonds, or over-weights international equities—it has to adjust while still maintaining the same risk levels.

This works like a scale as far as risk and reward. CLS believes that if it moves a weight on the scale too far on one side, the scale goes out of balance. To counter that, CLS has to move something in the portfolio closer to the middle of the risk category so the portfolio is close to being in balance. CLS portfolio managers go over their risk with each client and compare it to the degree of risk they can handle. "In good markets, bad markets, in good economic times, and in bad economic times, we believe in maintaining that risk level," Clarke says. "That doesn't mean we maintain a passive approach to the investments, but we maintain the proper risk level."

Because of risk budgeting, Clarke says, the company has to be careful in what to buy. Actively managed mutual funds don't work for the company. An active manager can make significant adjustments in his portfolio, and this can throw off the amount of risk CLS wants to take. "Quite honestly," Clarke says, "even if it's not an actively managed mutual fund, any mutual fund that has the ability to go from large-cap to mid-cap, or go from mid-cap to small-cap, kind of throws off our measurements when we go to measuring risk."

ETFs Fit the CLS Investments Method

That is why CLS Investments likes ETFs. ETFs give the ability to purchase passively managed investments, and the company knows exactly what it's buying. The company understands the type of investment it makes when buying, for example, a large-cap ETF or when buying a Malaysia ETF. Understanding what it is buying allows the company to calculate the amount of risk in that investment based upon the holdings, and then it can surgically allocate that risk into portfolios. It doesn't have to worry about the manager's style drifting or significantly changing the holdings, because it is an ETF based on an index.

CLS uses a wide range of asset classes, and sometimes it uses individual bonds, and sometimes it uses individual stocks. But basically, the portfolio managers are not stock pickers, and they are better at managing the markets, analyzing asset classes, and measuring the risk of the asset classes in their entirety, and then mixing the asset classes into client portfolios to maintain the risk level in the portfolio. Clarke says ETFs "give us that broad diversification and it's a passive investment that allows us to actively manage a portfolio, and that helps us in measuring that risk."

Sometimes cash in a portfolio can help balance risk. "If we have cash in portfolios," Clarke says, "and from time to time, we will have a position in cash that is a risk-free asset, and in order to maintain a client's appropriate risk level, we have to purchase a more aggressive asset class to counter that cash position." A CLS client is measured from 0 to 100 on a risk budget, and if a client is measured at a 70, for example, that client would have a mix of stocks, bonds, commodities, real estate, and other asset classes, including cash. To counter the low-cash risk, CLS purchases more aggressive asset classes, such as increasing holdings in value equities, technology equities, or other assets.

Matching a Client's Needs to Goals

"We try, as best as we possibly can, to measure the amount of risk that a client is willing to take in the market, and give them a realistic expectation as to what their returns can be, in the long run, given their risk level," Clarke says. What is difficult about managing money, he says, is helping the client understand that the amount of risk he wants or is willing to take may or may not accomplish his financial objectives.

Clarke says one of the difficult aspects of investing is keeping clients objective and realistic as to what their investments can accomplish and not get carried away with unrealistic goals. "All too often," he says, "investors come to us and to other money managers and say, 'I have a $100,000, and in the next 18 months, I need to use the majority of it to fund my grandchild's education. In order to do that I need an 18 percent return.'"

Those goals and objectives don't always line up with what is possible and prudent, Clarke says. He believes it is important that clients understand that investments are for the long term, and cash and income are for the short term. Being able to separate that and help clients to see what they are able or not able to do is critical.

For the client who wanted an 18 percent return over 18 months, or other potential clients like that, Clarke says, "We don't take them. We are able to turn down business, or at least if they insist on that, we are able to state our case about what would be prudent, and why." He says that this kind of money, the kind that will be needed in the next 18 months for a college education, belongs in a savings account.

CLS builds a portfolio around as much financial situation information as a potential client shares. The easy part is managing the money, and Clarke says, "The difficult part is aligning the client's goals with what the money is capable of doing."

Measuring Risk for Client Portfolios

"Whether there is another terrorist threat, or Spain or Greece collapse, or whether the U.S. economy picks up or doesn't pick up, from a money management standpoint, we continue to plug along," Clarke says. CLS continues to measure the amount of risk that is in the marketplace, and makes sure that its clients' portfolios adhere to the proper risk level. CLS does not predict things such as the future price of gold or whether real estate will come back or not come back, but rather invests in many asset classes according to its clients' risk levels.

Commodities have a place in the CLS universe of investments and act as a diversification tool to traditional asset classes. "Just like any other asset class, commodities carry a risk factor," Clarke says, "and we're considering that risk to be pretty high." Clarke says that just because risk is high doesn't mean that an asset class won't go higher, and if risk is low that doesn't mean that the asset class won't go lower. Risk in each asset class changes, and CLS measures that risk, and if it wants to have a piece of risk, it buys the risky asset class. It stays diversified and knows its risk appetite, and if it wants to have a sliver in commodities, for example, it buys and assigns a risk score to the commodity. Because of the rise in the price of commodities, CLS assigns a higher risk budget score to it than it did ten years ago.

CLS's analysts monitor risk levels of each asset class and use all classes in its attempt to stay diversified. Clarke says, "You want to have a little bit across all areas, but you want to measure the amount of risk so you don't get your portfolio tilted too far to one direction. And a buy-and-hold strategy is not measuring the amount of risk." If a client wants 10 percent in real estate at all times in a buy-and-hold strategy, that won't work, because the risk in holding real estate changes over time. Clarke says, "Some might argue that the amount of risk in real estate is a lot lower than it was three years ago."

CLS determines the amount of risk in each asset class, and then make adjustments so that its clients' risk level is constant. The result is that its clients' holdings in equities, bonds, commodities, real estate, and other asset classes will not stay constant. "We look at all those categories in building our clients' portfolios and then measure the risk in those categories and make changes from time to time. We're not speculating that gold is going to go up, and we're going to move our clients into it, or silver's going to go down and we're going to move our clients out of it. We're more concerned about the amount of risk in that asset class."

Sage Advisory Services, Ltd. Co.

Robert G. Smith, AIF, CIMC (President and CIO)
www.sageadvisory.com

Sage's services are centered on aligning the safety, liquidity, income, tax sensitivity, and return expectations of its clients with their risk budgets. Sage tailors portfolios according to the distinctive needs of each client and uses its risk control disciplines for downside protection. AUM as of June 30, 2011 is $9.5 billion.

Sage's Investment Strategies for Equity and Fixed Income

Sage Advisory Services, Ltd. Co. ("Sage"), headquartered in Austin, Texas, serves the institutional and private client marketplace with traditional and liability-driven fixed-income asset management, and tactical ETF strategies. With more than a decade of experience utilizing ETFs, Sage was one of the first investment managers to launch an all-ETF strategy back in 2002. In addition to the Core Plus Fixed Income and All Cap Equity Plus strategies, Sage offers a series of total portfolio solutions that have a target-risk orientation.

Its investment and research process is built around the forward-looking tactical management of the big market segment decisions, as it believes market segment allocation decisions have the biggest impact on portfolio performance and risk management. Sage feels that the depth of its investment team and experience in delivering solutions to the institutional marketplace gives it a very unique perspective about the way that the tactical ETF strategies are managed.

Research Analysis Used for Fixed Income and Equity Portfolios

For fixed income, Sage combines fundamental economic and quantitative security analysis in a detailed investment process and specifically identifies those sectors of the broad, fixed-income markets that offer optimal gross risk-adjusted returns, and also offer after-tax returns over a rolling six-month horizon, that are within a client's risk constraints.

The company's tactical equity-investment process is quantitatively driven, using proprietary models to help in each of three primary allocation decisions. The decisions include: equity weighting versus cash; market segment weighting, which involves market cap size, including large-, mid-, and small-; style, which is growth and value; international versus domestic; and, alternative inclusions, such as commodities and REITs.

Sage Used ETFs to Expand from a Traditional Fixed-Income Management Firm

Robert Smith, president of Sage Advisory Services, started Sage in the late 1990s. From the beginning, the company was interested in ETFs when the American Stock Exchange first launched them. "Sage was a fixed-income shop," Smith says, "but there was demand from our fixed-income clients to have us manage the equity side of their allocation. We believed that the best equity solution for our clients would be one that was cost-efficient, that had high degrees of liquidity, and would allow us the flexibility to move into and out of the equity market on more of a tactical basis." Sage believed that ETFs helped fill this need, but became convinced of that after visiting the

AMEX back in 1998 to learn more about the ETF structure and inner workings of the ETF market.

It became clear to Smith that ETFs would be the concept that would take over from mutual funds quickly, and that ETFs were the way that most of the comingled community was going to go. Smith saw many advantages of ETFs and also thought at the time that no matter if they were in a bull market or bear market, the vast majority of active stock selectors were not capable of consistently beating the market indexes.

ETFs Were Efficient for Big or Small Clients

Smith saw that ETFs had significant viability, particularly because they were convenient for investors to buy 1 share, or 100 shares, or 1,000 shares of ETFs. There was no loss of investment efficiency in terms of scalability. That was good for Smith's small clients and for his larger clients, and Sage, when possible, prefers to apply and deliver a consistent strategy for all of its clients. Sage started to write about ETFs to inform clients and others in 1998, and many people thought at first that ETFs seemed strange.

Sage felt, nevertheless, that ETFs were the wave of the future. Sage's use of ETFs was from the perspective of a fixed-income manager, and so, when developing tactical allocations, it leaned hard on macro-economic analysis. Smith says its top-down analysis of economic conditions combined with a fundamental and relative valuation of the different market segments gave Sage insight into the direction of the equity markets.

Smith thought if Sage could identify the healthy and weak parts of the economy and combine that perspective with fundamental analysis, it could construct asset-allocation strategies that would allow it to make good investments for their clients. "Problem was," Smith says, "we had to wait for the ETF market to develop, mature, and evolve into the strategies that we thought were important.

Deciding on the Best Way to Invest Using ETFs

It was clear to Smith that what he had to do was make sure he had the "right" over-weight in the "right" market segments and under-weight, or avoidance of the market segments that were not going to work. Smith says, "We believed that stock selection didn't bring much to the game and that active and inactive stock selection didn't add a lot on a longer-term time horizon, so why focus much time and attention on that?"

Although Smith heard from investors and consultants that good stock selectors were still desired, Smith thought it didn't make sense to look for stock pickers that could outperform. Sage believed that building asset-allocation strategies based on getting the big asset-allocation decisions right was a much more effective way to add value for clients and ETFs were the best vehicle to execute on this belief.

Smith says that by 2002, as the ETF creators continued introducing new securities and fleshing out the style boxes, Sage had the tools necessary to build one of the first all-ETF strategies, which was an all-cap equity mandate. "And then our macro-economic overlay would drive the process so that we wouldn't be concerned about stocks; we would not be primarily concerned about industry focus. Rather, it would be the other way around: top-down, get the economic call right first, understand the fundamentals of each market segment, and position the portfolio based on the allocation that appeared most favorable over the next 3–6 months."

From this standpoint, Sage concluded that it would capitalize by investing in those quadrants of the equity market based on their historical analysis. Smith says it was easy to go back in time and see when the prevailing winds would blow in the economy. For example, Sage would look at when large-cap does better than small-cap or when growth does better than value, in terms of the prevailing economic setting, from a macro standpoint.

Sage went back several decades and identified those periods of time, and captured those cyclical effects in its ETF selection, which was the first step in setting its strategy.

Sage Became a Tactical Manager

Sage put together a number of different economic screens that enables it to understand when to over-weight and under-weight based on the macro-economic, forward-looking call.

"The other thing that everybody did in asset allocation up to that point was mean variance optimization, which was the dominant theme," Smith says. "You always had to have exposure to every part of the style box. We thought that was bunk. Driving down the future highway looking through the rear-view mirror gave you little benefit, in our view," Smith says. Also Sage thought that having something in everything was of little benefit.

Sage became "decidedly tactical, in the truest sense of the word," Smith says. For long periods of time, Sage might not have any small-cap, for instance. For long periods of time, it might not have one growth component in its portfolios. It might have only mid-cap or over-weight mid-cap instead of small-cap or large-cap.

Smith says that Sage has a "fully fleshed out, macro-economically driven model that attacks all the nine parts of the asset class style box, and determines what areas you're going to be in and not in. We are purists, we don't mix cats and dogs, and only work with ETFs that are built upon and framed out according to the tenants of market-cap weighted indexes."

Getting Better Yields by Investing in Global Fixed Income

In the early days of ETF innovation, the equity and alternative asset classes dominated. By 2006 and 2007, ETF creators expanded into fixed-income ETFs. Sage vice president Michael D. Walton says, "It's our perspective that the most important advancements in the

ETF space over the last six or seven years have been the development of ETFs to represent all areas of the global fixed-income market."

At that time, Sage was able to take its institutional fixed-income process, typically implemented with individual bonds, and replicate that process in an all-ETF format. Walton says, "Not only did the use of fixed-income ETFs allow us to offer our strategies at much lower minimums, but ETFs offer some very unique trading efficiencies compared to individual bonds."

"Investors typically don't take advantage of the entire global bond market, and that is one of the things that ETFs allow you to do very efficiently. You can get tactical exposure to high-yield debt, emerging markets debt, international treasuries, and Treasury Inflation-Protected Securities (TIPS). The point is, you can efficiently get exposure to non-core sectors of the market using ETFs."

Using ETFs to Gain Desired Asset Class Exposure

Sage has been tactical in its fixed-income strategies, especially with non-core fixed income. As far as trading in and out of different asset classes using ETFs, Smith says, "It is very easy to move in and out of the different market segments using ETFs, but it's very important to note that proper due diligence of the ETF and underlying index is critical.

"Our clients appreciate our ability to build asset allocations and make tactical allocation changes. But it is just as important that our clients appreciate that we've been evaluating and researching ETFs and the underlying indexes for the better part of 12 years."

INDEX

FINANCIAL TIMES

In an increasingly competitive world, it is quality
of thinking that gives an edge—an idea that opens new
doors, a technique that solves a problem, or an insight
that simply helps make sense of it all.

We work with leading authors in the various arenas
of business and finance to bring cutting-edge thinking
and best-learning practices to a global market.

It is our goal to create world-class print publications
and electronic products that give readers
knowledge and understanding that can then be
applied, whether studying or at work.

To find out more about our business
products, you can visit us at www.ftpress.com.